# BIBLE STUDY GUIDE

From the Bible-teaching ministry of

*Charles R. Swindoll*

INSIGHT FOR LIVING

Charles R. Swindoll is a graduate of Dallas Theological Seminary and has served as senior pastor of the First Evangelical Free Church of Fullerton, California, since 1971. Chuck's radio program, "Insight for Living," began in 1979. In addition to his church and radio ministries, Chuck enjoys writing. He has authored numerous books and booklets on a variety of subjects.

Based on the outlines and transcripts of Chuck's sermons, the study guide text is co-authored by Bryce Klabunde, a graduate of Biola University and Dallas Theological Seminary. He also wrote the Living Insights sections.

**Editor in Chief:**
Cynthia Swindoll

**Coauthor of Text:**
Bryce Klabunde

**Assistant Editor:**
Wendy Peterson

**Copy Editors:**
Deborah Gibbs
Cheryl Gilmore
Karene Wells

**Designer:**
Gary Lett

**Publishing System Specialist:**
Bob Haskins

**Director, Communications Division:**
Deedee Snyder

**Manager, Creative Services:**
Alene Cooper

**Project Supervisor:**
Susan Nelson

**Print Production Manager:**
John Norton

**Printer:**
Sinclair Printing Company

Unless otherwise identified, all Scripture references are from the New American Standard Bible, © The Lockman Foundation 1960, 1962, 1963, 1968, 1971, 1972, 1973, 1975, 1977. Used by permission.

Current guide coauthored by Bryce Klabunde:
   © 1993 Charles R. Swindoll. All rights reserved.
Guide edited by Bill Watkins:
   © 1985 Charles R. Swindoll. All rights reserved.
Original outlines and transcripts:
   © 1984 Charles R. Swindoll. All rights reserved.

An effort has been made to locate sources and obtain permission where necessary for the quotations used in this book. In the event of any unintentional omission, a modification will gladly be incorporated in future printings.

ISBN 0-8499-8463-7
Printed in the United States of America.

COVER DESIGN: Nina Paris
COVER PHOTOGRAPHY: Neo Photo Inc.
COVER BACKGROUND FABRIC: Used by permission of Kravet Fabrics, Inc., Bethpage, Long Island, New York.

# CONTENTS

# INTRODUCTION

Dear Member of the Family:

Here is a unique series of studies. Maybe you have heard of such a project, but I never had before I undertook it. For the longest time, I have observed the family from the obvious perspective: husbands and wives, children and parents, etc. But then it dawned on me one day that we have been overlooking some equally important folks for many, many years.

So this series brings to the forefront those in the family who have been obscure long enough—people like the single parent, the handicapped, the unmarried, the orphan, the grandparent, the childless couple, and on and on. I think it will be encouraging for you to discover how beautifully God's Word speaks to all in the family.

I hope each study causes you to realize just how broad and varied the family of God really is. It takes all of us to make the "forever family" portrait complete.

Chuck Swindoll

# PUTTING TRUTH
## INTO ACTION

Knowledge apart from application falls short of God's desire for His children. He wants us to apply what we learn so that we will change and grow. This study guide was prepared with these goals in mind. As you go through the following pages, we hope your desire to discover biblical truth will grow as your understanding of God's Word increases, and that you will be encouraged to apply what you've learned.

To assist you in your study, we've included a section called 🌹 Living Insights at the end of each lesson. These exercises will challenge you to study further and to think of specific ways to put your discoveries into action.

There are many ways to use this guide—in personal devotions, group studies, discussions with friends and family, and Sunday school classes. And, of course, it's an ideal study aid when you're listening to its corresponding "Insight for Living" radio series.

To benefit most from this study guide, we would encourage you to consider it a spiritual journal. That's why we've included space in the Living Insights for recording your thoughts and discoveries. We hope you'll return to those sections often for review and encouragement as you continue to grow in your walk with Christ.

*Bryce Klabunde*

Bryce Klabunde
Coauthor of Text
Author of Living Insights

A
_Family_
A L B U M

## Chapter 1

# MEET THE MOTHER
# OF MOSES
### Exodus 1:8–2:10

The boy sat on the couch next to his grandmother, peering at the family photo album bridged across their laps. "Here's your great-grandfather, and look, here's your grandfather when he was your age," she said, pointing to a yellowed photograph. "My, if he doesn't look like you!"

As if into a mirror, the boy stared at the knickered lad whose resemblance he bore.

"When your grandpa came to America, all he and his parents had were the clothes on their backs and a few cents in their pockets . . ."

This wasn't the first time Grandma had told him the family story from her book. Still, the boy listened closely, absorbing the images as she gingerly turned the pages. To anyone else, these were just nameless faces, but to him they were legends, courageous overcomers—his heroes.

In a way, the Bible is like this family album. Images of heroes and heroines who rose from obscurity fill its pages too. There's Jephthah, the street kid God turned into a judge; Amos, the field laborer who became a prophet; David, the shepherd boy who became king; Esther, an exiled Jewess who became a Persian queen; and Joseph, the rejected brother and slave who became prime minister of Egypt.

In this study, we'll be like the boy with his grandmother. We'll peer at a few photographs in the Book, listen closely to each one's story, and learn about ourselves in the process. As we begin, take a look at this first picture: it's of a mother nursing her baby, a baby born in poverty—a baby named Moses.

## Origin of Moses: A Ghetto in Goshen

Moses' mother often slips our notice when we consider the life of

1

the great patriarch. Certainly, her name, Jochebed (see Exod. 6:20), is not as recognizable as, say, Sarah's or Rachel's. Yet, more than any other person, she set the foundation for Moses' valiant faith. And she did this at a time in Israel's history when the Hebrew people were living out a horrid existence in an Egyptian ghetto known as Goshen.

### Affliction and Oppression

Years earlier Jacob and his clan had settled in Goshen. Under the care of his son, Prime Minister Joseph, Jacob's descendants quickly multiplied and, in time, "became exceedingly mighty, so that the land was filled with them" (1:7b).

Eventually, however,

> a new king arose over Egypt, who did not know Joseph. And he said to his people, "Behold, the people of the sons of Israel are more and mightier than we. Come, let us deal wisely with them, lest they multiply and in the event of war, they also join themselves to those who hate us, and fight against us, and depart from the land." So they appointed taskmasters over them to afflict them with hard labor. And they built for Pharaoh storage cities, Pithom and Raamses. (vv. 8–11)

Imagine the people's distress under this new king. For years they had enjoyed freedom and prosperity while living along the fertile Nile. Then without warning, like the Jews in World War II, they were stripped of their rights when the gestapo-like taskmasters raided their homes and businesses. Suddenly, their young men became beasts of burden; their women, defenseless chattels; their neighborhoods, impoverished ghettos.

Yet, the resilient Hebrews thrived, for

> the more they afflicted them, the more they multiplied and the more they spread out, so that [the Egyptians] were in dread of the sons of Israel. And the Egyptians compelled the sons of Israel to labor rigorously; and they made their lives bitter with hard labor in mortar and bricks and at all kinds of labor in the field, all their labors which they rigorously imposed on them. (vv. 12–14)

How the Hebrews must have languished under their cruel masters! F. B. Meyer described the average man as toiling day after day

> beneath the burning sun, returning often with bleeding wounds torn open by the scourge, and inclined to question the very existence of God and his character for mercy.[1]

Surely, God would bring them a deliverer . . . wouldn't He? Maybe one of their own sons would be the man. That hope was their only flickering candle in the oppressive Egyptian darkness.

### Midwives and Murder

But even that tiny light threatened to disappear when Pharaoh wickedly determined to curb the ever-increasing Hebrew population.

> The king of Egypt spoke to the Hebrew midwives, one of whom was named Shiphrah, and the other was named Puah; and he said, "When you are helping the Hebrew women to give birth and see them upon the birthstool, if it is a son, then you shall put him to death; but if it is a daughter, then she shall live." (vv. 15–16)

*Hebrew midwives* can be translated "midwives of the Hebrews," indicating that they may have been Egyptians assigned to deliver the Hebrews' babies. Fortunately, the king's covert plot failed, because

> the midwives feared God, and did not do as the king of Egypt had commanded them, but let the boys live. So the king of Egypt called for the midwives, and said to them, "Why have you done this thing, and let the boys live?" And the midwives said to Pharaoh, "Because the Hebrew women are not as the Egyptian women; for they are vigorous, and they give birth before the midwife can get to them." So God was good to the midwives, and the people multiplied, and became very mighty. And it came about because the midwives feared God, that He established households for them. (vv. 17–21)

---

1. F. B. Meyer, *Moses: The Servant of God* (Grand Rapids, Mich.: Zondervan Publishing House, 1953), p. 14.

The midwives' faith revealed God's presence in this oppressive scene. Despite Pharaoh's barbarous plan, He was in control.

Frustrated once, Pharaoh intensified his brutal prejudice and designed another plot—this one unashamedly overt.

> Then Pharaoh commanded all his people, saying, "Every son who is born you are to cast into the Nile, and every daughter you are to keep alive." (v. 22)

The order rang out: Kill all newborn Hebrew sons. We can only imagine the horror of such an edict—the nighttime raids, the hateful voices, the screaming mothers, the shrieking babies. But in the midst of this terror, we meet steadfast Jochebed and her husband, Amram.

## The Home of Moses: A Hovel of Hope

Jochebed and Amram already have two children: Aaron, age three (see 7:7); and Miriam, possibly a young teenager. One day Jochebed tells her husband she is pregnant again. What if it's a boy? What would they do?

### Courageous Protection

> And the woman conceived and bore a son; and when she saw that he was beautiful, she hid him for three months. (2:2)

In the New Testament, the letter to the Hebrews also notes this curious comment on Moses' beauty and includes further insight into his parents' faith:

> By faith Moses, when he was born, was hidden for three months by his parents, because they saw he was a beautiful child; and they were not afraid of the king's edict. (Heb. 11:23)

More than just a cute baby, Moses apparently bore the Almighty's special touch (see Acts 7:20), and his parents saw it clearly.[2] Confident in God and unintimidated by Pharaoh's ever-present police, Jochebed and Amram hide their son as long as they can. Eventually, though, they need to devise another plan.

2. According to F. B. Meyer, the ancient historian Josephus wrote "that a dream announced to Amram that Moses would be the deliverer of his people." *Moses*, p. 17. Whether the dream ever occurred, it is apparent that his parents knew God had a purpose for Moses and that they should do whatever they could to preserve his life.

## Creative Scheme

With Moses now three months old, Jochebed knows that simply hiding him will no longer work. So, using all of her creativity and resourcefulness, she develops the following scheme:

> But when she could hide him no longer, she got him a wicker basket and covered it over with tar and pitch. Then she put the child into it, and set it among the reeds by the bank of the Nile. And his sister stood at a distance to find out what would happen to him. Then the daughter of Pharaoh came down to bathe at the Nile, with her maidens walking alongside the Nile; and she saw the basket among the reeds and sent her maid, and she brought it to her.
>
> When she opened it, she saw the child, and behold, the boy was crying. And she had pity on him and said, "This is one of the Hebrews' children." Then his sister said to Pharaoh's daughter, "Shall I go and call a nurse for you from the Hebrew women, that she may nurse the child for you?" And Pharaoh's daughter said to her, "Go ahead." So the girl went and called the child's mother. Then Pharaoh's daughter said to her, "Take this child away and nurse him for me and I shall give you your wages." (Exod. 2:3–9a)

Jochebed's ingenious plan worked wonderfully. What was most remarkable was her ability to do the unthinkable as a mother . . . give up her baby. How could she push that basket, with its precious cargo, into the unknown waters of the Nile? As F. B. Meyer observed,

> [she was] fighting a mother's natural anxiety by a faith which had enclasped the very arm of the living God, who could not fail her, though the heavens should fall, or the pyramids be hurled into the broad bosom of the Nile. That is faith. Can we wonder at the faith of the man who was born of such a mother, and nurtured in such a home?[3]

3. Meyer, Moses, p. 18.

## Concentrated Nurture

God honored Jochebed's faith by allowing her to nurture Moses during his formative years—and Pharaoh's daughter even paid her to do it!

> So the woman took the child and nursed him. And the child grew, and she brought him to Pharaoh's daughter, and he became her son. And she named him Moses, and said, "Because I drew him out of the water." (vv. 9b–10)

How long was Moses in his mother's care? Maybe five years at the most. During that sweet period, Jochebed must have poured her faith into his soul every moment. While he nursed, she sang him God's love songs; while she prayed, he learned his first words. She gave him her energy, her effort, and her counsel.

Referring to this concentrated nurture, J. Oswald Sanders once observed:

> In that home [Moses] learned two vitally important lessons. From his parents he learned *faith in God*. . . . From them, too, he imbibed a *fearless courage*. Their faith transcended their fear of the king's wrath. The courage of the parents produced moral bravery in the son.[4]

Can so much be taught to such a young child? The letter to the Hebrews subtly confirms that it can. Notice the connection between Moses and his parents:

- "[Jochebed and Amram] were not afraid of the king's edict" (Heb. 11:23b).

- "By faith [Moses] left Egypt, not fearing the wrath of the king" (v. 27a).

Where did he learn this courageous faith? At home as a child.

## A Few of the Principles That Fit Today

Our picture of Jochebed tenderly nursing Baby Moses portrays several truths about families.

---

4. J. Oswald Sanders, *Robust in Faith* (Chicago, Ill.: Moody Press, 1965), p. 58.

First, *it's possible to overestimate the impact of environment.* Think of young Moses' environment: the rugged hut, the social upheaval, the prejudice, the violent oppression. Yet God overruled it all. In His sovereignty, He drew greatness out of the ash heap. Although we may see our environment as a handicap, God is not limited by it, and we are never disqualified from experiencing His life-changing grace.

Second, *it's possible to underestimate the importance of parenting.* Jochebed's brief presence influenced Moses' entire life. Certainly, her sacrifices were painful, but her faith and courage replicated themselves in his life—ultimately resulting in freedom for their people. Her message to us today is: Don't give up when the stresses of parenting seem overwhelming; it's worth it in the end.

Third, *regardless of the odds, a faithful model is valuable.* When the evil of the world seems unconquerable, we can be tempted to think, Why bother—what difference does my life make? At times like these, remember Jochebed; she simply believed in the Lord and in her child, little realizing that her faith would be speaking to us today.

Fourth, *because of life's pressures, an available mother is essential.* Without being open and available to God, Jochebed would not have had the strength to withstand Pharaoh's pressures. But because she held fast to her faith, she was able to preserve her baby's life and nurture him in his formative years. We, too, can only give something to our children after we have received something from the Lord.

In the few years God has given you to nurture your children, what will you give them? If you give them yourself and your faith in God, you'll be giving the greatest gifts of all.

## 🌹 *Living Insights*                              STUDY ONE

Call to mind the faces in your family album. There's your sister—she's a single mom trying to raise three kids on a teacher's salary. Then there's Uncle Howard—his wife died ten years ago, and all his children have moved away. And Mom and Dad, of course—they live nearby, which is great . . . most of the time. There's your younger brother and his wife—still no kids, and they're considering adoption.

Now you come to your picture. Are you single? Married? Do you have a disabled child? Stepchildren? Are you childless? A young parent? A parent of teenagers? A parent with an empty nest?

All of these relationships and configurations make up today's families—families with specific and complex problems.

As we begin this study of the various families found in the Bible, take a moment to write down the challenges your family faces.

_____

_____

_____

_____

As parents, Jochebed and Amram faced tremendous stress from Pharaoh's murderous mandate, yet they reacted with courage. Our prayer is that you will discover that same faith as you proceed through this study guide. Right now, will you also begin in prayer, laying before the Lord your "Pharaoh situation" and asking Him for direction and wisdom in your study of the Scriptures?

## 🌹 Living Insights

One word, perhaps above all others, stands out when we think of mothers: *giving*. From the time a precious child is conceived, a mother's giving begins. She gives of her own body in the growth of her forming child. She gives birth. She gives nourishment. She gives attention. She gives baths. She gives care. She gives hugs. She gives toys. She gives spankings. She gives haircuts. She gives Band-Aids. She gives clean clothes. She gives her hand for chewed gum. She gives allowances. She gives permission. She gives rides. She gives advice. She gives her car—until midnight.

You get the picture. Mothers give a lot.

But where do they get all that they give? Did God endow mothers with a self-replenishing supply of resources, a naturally limitless capacity to invest themselves in their children? No, as nice as that would be, He did not. He made them just like any other mortal: with a need to come away, be restored, be filled.

Jochebed seemed to know this; she stole away with God, fed her faith, relied on His help to cope with the pressures of her world.

Moms, are you following in Jochebed's footsteps? Are you making yourself available to God, taking time out to be replenished by His presence? Or are you trying to feed your family from an empty plate? Write down what you are currently doing to restock your physical, emotional, and spiritual supplies.

_____

_____

_____

Do your cupboards seem a tad bare? What's been overlooked in all the hectic demands to give?

_____

_____

Right now, moms—and here's where you can help, dads—think of at least three specific ways you can let God replenish you. One idea might be sleeping in on Saturday and letting Dad get the kids' breakfast. Maybe you could join that Bible study you've been thinking about. Or perhaps it's as simple as just sitting down while you're eating lunch. Take some time to think this over; then write down your ideas.

1._____

_____

2._____

_____

3._____

_____

Now choose one and put it into practice immediately! And don't allow any guilty feelings to talk you out of it. Remember: Because of life's pressures, an available mother is essential.

Chapter 2

# A COUPLE MIGHTILY USED OF GOD

### Acts 18:1–3, 18–21, 24–28

O f all the photo albums accumulated by a family, the favorite has to be the wedding album. Dreamy little girls love to gaze at Mommy in her lacy, fairy-tale wedding dress. Boys like to laugh at Dad's thick hair, sideburns, and purple velvet bow tie. Of course, it's Mom and Dad's favorite too: "How young we were!" "I was so nervous!" "It seems like yesterday."

Likewise, God's biblical family album offers several wedding pictures we can pore over. One is of a couple God used mightily: Aquila and Priscilla. Their marriage provides us with a model of "couple power"—a picture of the impact couples can make for Christ.

What gives couples their unique strengths? Let's turn to some wise words of Solomon to find out.

## Easily Forgotten Benefits of Being a Married Couple

As we blow the dust off Solomon's ancient book of Ecclesiastes, we'll discover four benefits of togetherness that we can apply to marriage. The first, shown in chapter 4, verse 9, is *mutual effort*.

> Two are better than one because they have a
> good return for their labor.

The work of making a living, handling pressures, and dealing with disappointments is easier when shared as a couple.

Also, couples can enjoy *mutual support*.

> For if either of them falls, the one will lift up his
> companion. But woe to the one who falls when there
> is not another to lift him up. (v. 10)

When one partner is emotionally down, the other can usually bring back a smile with an affirming hug and a listening ear.

Third, marriages can be a source of *mutual encouragement*.

> Furthermore, if two lie down together they keep

10

warm, but how can one be warm alone? (v. 11)

There's nothing quite as comforting as the warmth of your mate beside you on a cold winter's night, assuring you that everything will be all right.

Finally, *mutual strength* is available to the couple.

> And if one can overpower him who is alone, two
> can resist him. (v. 12a)

Rearing children, surviving financial setbacks, enduring illness, or making tough decisions is difficult alone. But a married couple can pray for one another and stand together, facing life's challenges with added strength.

As we turn from Ecclesiastes to Acts 18, we'll see that Aquila and Priscilla undoubtedly enjoyed these four benefits of married life. And we might even say they were experiencing a fifth benefit to being a couple: mutual ministry.

## A Certain Couple Who Ministered

We first become acquainted with this husband-and-wife team when they join up with the apostle Paul during his second missionary journey. Paul had just come from Athens, where he had the opportunity to speak to the intellectual Areopagus philosophers.[1] After all his efforts, however, only a smattering of Athenians became Christians.

Disappointed, Paul finally left Athens for Corinth, hoping for a better response to his message. But when he arrived in that bawdy port city, he was faced with open prostitution and a seedy street life unparalleled in any other city he'd seen. With little money, no place to stay, and no friends among these intimidating strangers, Paul's heart must have ached with loneliness.

Years later, in his letter to the Corinthians, he admitted,

> I was with you in weakness and in fear and in much
> trembling. (1 Cor. 2:3)

---

1. *Areopagus* may have meant "Hill of Ares," referring to the Greek god of war. It is also known as "Mars' Hill," the equivalent Roman god. In Paul's day, the Court of the Areopagus "exercised a general censorship in matters of religion and education." Interestingly, the Supreme Court of Greece today is called the Areopagus. A. Rupprecht, "Areopagus," *The Zondervan Pictorial Encyclopedia of the Bible*, gen. ed. Merrill C. Tenney (Grand Rapids, Mich.: Zondervan Publishing House, Regency Reference Library, 1976), vol. 1, pp. 298–99.

Then, unexpectedly, he met Aquila and Priscilla.

### Ministry and Gifts

> And he found a certain Jew named Aquila, a native
> of Pontus, having recently come from Italy with his
> wife Priscilla, because Claudius had commanded all
> the Jews to leave Rome. He came to them, and be-
> cause he was of the same trade, he stayed with them
> and they were working; for by trade they were tent-
> makers. (Acts 18:2–3)

God brought this couple across Paul's path just when he needed
them most. Mere coincidence? Hardly. In fact, God's sovereign hand
was at work months earlier when the emperor's edict forced them
out of Rome. At the time, they must have wondered, "Why us,
Lord? Why now? We like living in Rome." But God knew what He
was doing. Miles away, a tired missionary would need their companionship, and if they were willing, God wanted to use their home
as his haven.

How did Paul meet them? Again by "coincidence," he shared
their trade—tentmaking. We can imagine him wandering through
the bazaar one day, looking to buy a few supplies. Perhaps Aquila
and Priscilla were there too, haggling with a local merchant over
the price of fabric. Sidling up to them, Paul may have struck up a
conversation:

He: Are all the prices here so high?
They: They're terrible, aren't they?
He: In my hometown, the same material is half the price.
They: Where are you from? We're from Rome. . . .

In moments they were friends, and the couple graciously invited
Paul into their home. The text says simply, "He came to them" and
"he stayed with them."

Of course, they could have said to Paul, "Well, nice meeting
you. Hope you find a place to stay. Bye." They had to make a living
in this city too; how could they take in a stranger? Besides, having
been dumped out of their homeland, they had to think about their
own problems. A safer route would have been to draw the blinds,
lock the doors, and take care of themselves. Why reach out to others?

Despite these possible hesitations, they opened their home and
their hearts to Paul. And if they were not already Christians, they

also opened their lives to Paul's message and became followers of Christ.

Their story, however, does not end in Corinth. More than a year and a half later, Paul

> took leave of the brethren and put out to sea for Syria, *and with him were Priscilla and Aquila.* (v. 18b, emphasis added)

Such a willing attitude in this couple! They wanted God to use them wherever He chose, even if it meant once again uprooting their lives and launching out into the unknown.

When they arrived at Ephesus, Paul unexpectedly left for his third missionary journey (see v. 19a). For months, they had been absorbing Paul's teaching and methods, and now, with Paul away, it was time to begin their own pastoral ministry.

As the church in Ephesus grew under their leadership, Aquila and Priscilla had many opportunities to use their spiritual gifts. We've already seen at least five in action with Paul—encouragement, faith, helps, hospitality, and mercy. And now we'll see another, the gift of exhortation.

> Now a certain Jew named Apollos, an Alexandrian by birth, an eloquent man, came to Ephesus; and he was mighty in the Scriptures. This man had been instructed in the way of the Lord; and being fervent in spirit, he was speaking and teaching accurately the things concerning Jesus, being acquainted only with the baptism of John; and he began to speak out boldly in the synagogue. (vv. 24–26a)

From the world-renowned intellectual center of Alexandria came Apollos, every bit as bold and powerful as his name might suggest. But when he preached, he revealed an incomplete knowledge of Christ.[2] Aquila and Priscilla immediately picked up inconsistencies between his teaching and Paul's. Rather than quietly

---

2. "He did not understand the full orb of the gospel of grace completed with Jesus' crucifixion and resurrection. Neither did he know about the baptism of the Holy Spirit at Pentecost. The Spirit's powerful presence in the believer's life was a foreign concept to him." *The Strength of an Exacting Passion: A Study of Acts 18:18–28:31,* coauthored by Bryce Klabunde, from the Bible-teaching ministry of Charles R. Swindoll (Anaheim, Calif.: Insight for Living, 1992), p. 5.

scowling at him, embarrassing him in public, or whispering criticisms behind his back, "they took him aside and explained to him the way of God more accurately" (v. 26b).

Even though Apollos held all the academic credentials, he humbly accepted their private exhortations. Soon, with the full endorsement of Aquila and Priscilla, he felt ready to launch out on his own.

> And when he wanted to go across to Achaia, the brethren encouraged him and wrote to the disciples to welcome him; and when he had arrived, he helped greatly those who had believed through grace; for he powerfully refuted the Jews in public, demonstrating by the Scriptures that Jesus was the Christ. (vv. 27–28)

Later, Paul noted the effectiveness of Apollos' ministry in Corinth, saying that although he himself planted the church, Apollos watered it (see 1 Cor. 3:6a)—quite a tribute to Aquila and Priscilla's involvement in his life.

The Acts record leaves our couple in Ephesus, but at some point they returned to Rome, ministering to the believers there. Paul wrote in his letter to the Romans:

> Greet Prisca and Aquila, my fellow workers in Christ Jesus, who for my life risked their own necks, to whom not only do I give thanks, but also all the churches of the Gentiles; also greet the church that is in their house. (16:3–5a)

And by the end of Paul's life, they were again at work in Ephesus.

The Apostle wrote from his Roman prison to the young Ephesian pastor, Timothy: "Greet Prisca and Aquila" (2 Tim. 4:19a)—the couple who years earlier had befriended him on the lonely streets of Corinth.

### Rewards

By opening their lives to others, Aquila and Priscilla sacrificed the privacy and security other couples may have enjoyed. But in return, they reaped a harvest of rewards—rich memories, lasting friendships, and eternal benefits—the fruit of ministering as a couple. By being available to the Lord and willing to follow His way, we can enjoy those same rewards.

## For Couples Who Are Available and Willing Today

Eight simple words light the way toward mutual ministry as a couple. The first two are *give up*. Give up your grip on privacy. Give up your fear that if you open your doors, someone will discover your dirty dishes and unmade beds. Give up the words *me, mine,* and *more*. And give up your dream of isolating yourself from people with a Do Not Disturb sign on the door.

Next, *reach out*. Outside your garden wall lives a community of hurting people. There's the lonely college student, the exhausted single parent, the confused unwed mother, the widow, the divorcée, the neglected child. Through your marriage and your home, you have the power to help those who need to feel the security of a strong family.

Third, *take in*. Invite someone over for dessert, or include them in your picnic at the park. Take a widower along on your next fishing trip, or treat a single mom and her kids to lunch. The ways to take in others are endless. As a family, make specific plans to include others.

Finally, *start now*. You'll always have good reasons to keep your door closed: life is too frantic, the kids are too young, you're in transition, you're getting older, and on and on. If you don't start today, you'll put it off and probably miss out on some ripe opportunities to make a difference in someone's life.

### 🌹 *Living Insights* STUDY ONE

Have you ever thought of your home as a museum? Wander through the rooms sometime, and make a mental list of all the artifacts—a little vase that reminds you of someone dear, the photographs that recount your family history, the hand-knit afghan your grandmother made.

See, your house really is a museum of family history! Here's an idea as you think about adding new memories: display items that remind you of the people your family has helped—a snapshot of the Guatemalan boy your family sponsors each month or a small gift from the exchange student you hosted.

You can begin building these memories by reaching out to those in need. In what ways will you welcome others into your home this week?

_____

_____

What will you have to give up in order for the Lord to use you in these ways?

_____

_____

_____

Are you willing to let go of these things? If so, write out that desire and your commitment to allow the Lord to use you in others' lives.

_____

_____

_____

_____

_____

_____

The memories you accumulate by helping others will begin to fill your home with love's treasures.

## 🌹 *Living Insights* STUDY TWO

Ministering as a family reaps great rewards, but it does require balance and wisdom. To exercise your discernment muscles, examine the following situations and decide what the principal characters should do.

—————◆—————

To celebrate their first wedding anniversary, a young wife labors all day to prepare her husband's favorite meal. Stretching their tight budget, she buys top-quality steaks and broils them to perfection. She lays out their best dishes and sets a romantic mood in their tiny apartment with candles and soft music. Finally, her husband arrives home, and seeing what she has done, smiles gratefully at her. Two minutes after they sit down to eat, the doorbell rings. Their neighbors, a couple with continuing marital problems, need to talk. What should they do?

_____

_____

_____

—————◆———

A teenage girl moves in with her aunt and uncle's family because her parents have kicked her out of their house. When she arrives, she agrees to keep the family rules and to try to work things out with her parents. After a few weeks, tension begins to build between the girl and her three cousins. After two months of constant skirmishes and no resolution between the girl and her parents, the aunt and uncle can't stand the situation anymore. What should they do?

_____

_____

_____

—————◆———

The plight of the homeless has concerned this couple for a long time. One Sunday a family walks into their church, and it is obvious from their appearance that they have been living on the streets. After the service, the couple talks with them and discovers that they have no place to stay and that their baby needs medical attention. So the couple drives them to the local rescue mission and arranges to take them to the county clinic the next morning. A few days later, they receive a call from the father. He needs a ride to meet a friend about a possible job. Later in the week, he calls again, needing another ride and a little money to help them make it until the next government check. This continues until the couple feels overwhelmed with caring for this family's endless needs. What should they do?

_____

_____

_____

_____

Reaching out to others can lead to complicated, hard-to-resolve issues. Here are a few tips that will make dealing with these issues easier.

- When possible, join existing programs. For example, you can reach out to prisoners more effectively through involvement in a prison ministry rather than by yourself.

- Anticipate hardships. Before committing to help someone, think through all the possible stresses and plan in advance ways to overcome problems.

- Build a support network. Rely on other families in your church or on your pastor for advice and prayer—don't go it alone.

- Keep priorities. Even Jesus passed by needy people in order to accomplish a greater good. Sometimes no is the best answer.

Helping people can be difficult, but don't let that possibility discourage you from offering your hand to those in need. Instead, love others wisely so that, as Paul prayed,

> your love may abound still more and more in real knowledge and all discernment. (Phil. 1:9b)

## Chapter 3

# "GRANDPA UZZIAH": A STUDY IN CONTRASTS

*2 Chronicles 26:1–21*

In the eyes of many children, the wisest man on earth is their grandfather. Is there anything he doesn't know about? He can fix a bike chain, bait a fishing hook, or build a dollhouse. With a sniff of the air, he can even predict the weather. "Smells like rain," he'll say, and sure enough, it'll rain.

Another thing about grandfathers—they have big pockets where they keep important stuff handy, like a jackknife, an extra-large handkerchief, and lemon drops. Best of all, though, grandfathers have something most other adults tend to lack . . . time.

That is how many children view their grandfathers, and that's how it should be. In our study, we want to hold on to that childlike perspective, but we also want to be grown-up in our thinking. After all, grandfathers—and grandmothers—are only human. As one of Job's counselors, Elihu, observed,

> "The abundant in years may not be wise,
> Nor may elders understand justice." (Job 32:9)

Growing older doesn't guarantee growing wiser. In fact, the Bible is full of grandparent-age people who stumbled and fell: Noah, Abraham, Miriam, David, Moses, and many others. One man's tragic story stands as a particularly clear signpost of pitfalls ahead. This page of our family album shows a picture of a king wearing a splendid crown and displaying all the markings of well-earned success—yet in his eyes, there is a look of pain. His name is Uzziah.

## Orientation: Uzziah's Historical Background

Uzziah wielded the royal scepter in Judah during the divided kingdom period in Jewish history. Under Saul, David, and Solomon, the people had been united; but Solomon's son Rehoboam harshly treated the Jews in the north, causing a north-south split. The ten northern tribes retained the name Israel, while the two southern tribes adopted Judah as their name. The following charts illustrate the split and specify the reigns of King Uzziah's family.

# A Brief Chronology of Events and People

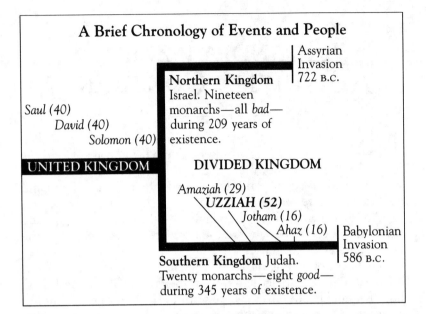

*Saul (40)*
*David (40)*
*Solomon (40)*

**UNITED KINGDOM**

**Northern Kingdom**
Israel. Nineteen
monarchs—all *bad*—
during 209 years of
existence.

Assyrian
Invasion
722 B.C.

**DIVIDED KINGDOM**

*Amaziah (29)*
**UZZIAH (52)**
*Jotham (16)*
*Ahaz (16)*

Babylonian
Invasion
586 B.C.

**Southern Kingdom** Judah.
Twenty monarchs—eight *good*—
during 345 years of existence.

## PERSONAL BIOGRAPHY
2 Chronicles 25–28

| Name | Age Began to Reign | Years Reigned | Age Died | Cause of Death | Relation to Uzziah |
|------|--------------------|---------------|----------|----------------|--------------------|
| Amaziah | 25 | 29 | 54 | Murder | His Father |
| **UZZIAH** | 16 | 52 | 68 | Leprosy | —— |
| Jotham | 25 | 16 | 41 | Natural (?) | His Son |
| Ahaz | 20 | 16 | 36 | Natural (?) | His Grandson |

## GENEALOGICAL CLARIFICATION

During the first sixteen years of Uzziah's life, his father, Amaziah, was the king. When Uzziah turned sixteen, he took his father's place on the throne.

When he was forty-three, his son Jotham was born. Jotham, like Uzziah, never knew a time when his father was not the king.

When Jotham was twenty-one, his son Ahaz was born . . . Uzziah's *grandson*. Since Jotham did not take the throne until he was twenty-five, Ahaz knew "Grandpa Uzziah" the final four years Uzziah was king. Ahaz was four years old when his dad, Jotham, became king.

Notice that Uzziah's father was murdered, resulting in Uzziah's assuming the throne at age sixteen. The crown must have weighed heavy on his young brow as thoughts of his father's ghastly death and worries of the kingdom pressed down on him. Would he have the qualities necessary to rule a nation? His father certainly hadn't modeled a kingly character, as summarized by the biblical chronicler:

> Amaziah was twenty-five years old when he became king, and he reigned twenty-nine years in Jerusalem. . . . And he did right in the sight of the Lord, *yet not with a whole heart.* (2 Chron. 25:1–2, emphasis added)

Amaziah was a compromising king, divided between his desire to please the Lord and his desire to please the people. As a result, he satisfied neither the Lord nor the nation, and eventually both turned against him. Late in his twenty-nine-year reign, he completely forsook Jehovah by worshiping foreign gods (see v. 14). From that fateful moment, the people

> conspired against him in Jerusalem, and he fled to Lachish; but they sent after him to Lachish and killed him there. Then they brought him on horses and buried him with his fathers in the city of Judah.
> And all the people of Judah took Uzziah, who was sixteen years old, and made him king in the place of his father Amaziah. . . . And he reigned fifty-two years in Jerusalem.[1] (25:27b–26:1, 3b)

## Observation: Uzziah's Admirable Achievements

Draped in his father's royal robe, the teenager must have shuddered as he heard the people shouting, "Long live King Uzziah!"

---

1. In this study, our perspective reflects the natural reading of the text, that sixteen-year-old Uzziah took over as king after his father's death. However, some commentators feel that this scenario presents several chronological problems when attempting to harmonize all the data on the kings of Judah and Israel. Edwin R. Thiele, in his book *The Mysterious Numbers of the Hebrew Kings* (Grand Rapids, Mich.: William B. Eerdmans Publishing Co., 1965), has reconstructed a viable chronology for the kings in which Uzziah is a vice-regent under Amaziah for about twenty-four years (p. 82). When Amaziah dies, he assumes the throne as the sole king at about age forty. For more information, see "2 Chronicles" by Eugene H. Merrill in *The Bible Knowledge Commentary*, Old Testament ed. (Wheaton, Ill.: Scripture Press Publications, Victor Books, 1985), pp. 513, 639.

Could he rule the nation any differently than his father? One thing was sure, he knew better than to make his father's mistakes. He must serve the Lord with his whole heart.

And as long as he did, he prospered.

### Spiritually

> He did right in the sight of the Lord. . . . And he continued to seek God in the days of Zechariah, who had understanding through the vision of God; and as long as he sought the Lord, God prospered him. (26:4a, 5)

Apparently, the prophet Zechariah influenced the young king, nurturing his faith. As a result, Uzziah was spiritually a success.

### Personally

Establishing his throne on this firm foundation, he began the task of rebuilding the kingdom after his father's disastrous reign.

> He built Eloth and restored it to Judah. . . . Moreover, Uzziah built towers in Jerusalem at the Corner Gate and at the Valley Gate and at the corner buttress and fortified them. And he built towers in the wilderness and hewed many cisterns, for he had much livestock, both in the lowland and in the plain. He also had plowmen and vinedressers in the hill country and the fertile fields, for he loved the soil. (vv. 2a, 9–10)

Because of his attention to and investment in his country,

> his fame extended to the border of Egypt, for he became very strong. . . . Hence his fame spread afar, for he was marvelously helped until he was strong. (vv. 8b, 15b)

In the polls, Uzziah's approval rating skyrocketed. But the king's ride to fame wasn't a solo flight—he was "marvelously helped" by the Lord of Hosts.

### Militarily

The Lord's hand in Uzziah's success is especially visible in the king's military exploits.

He went out and warred against the Philistines, and broke down the wall of Gath and the wall of Jabneh and the wall of Ashdod; and he built cities in the area of Ashdod and among the Philistines. And God helped him against the Philistines, and against the Arabians who lived in Gur-baal, and the Meunites. The Ammonites also gave tribute to Uzziah. . . . Moreover, Uzziah prepared for all the army shields, spears, helmets, body armor, bows and sling stones. And in Jerusalem he made engines of war invented by skillful men to be on the towers and on the corners, for the purpose of shooting arrows and great stones. (vv. 6–8a, 14–15a)

With the latest high-tech weaponry in place, the nation felt safe; morale was high, reminiscent of the days of King David. And Uzziah, with hair now gray, settled comfortably into the cushions of his secure throne.

## Corruption: Uzziah's Tragic Collapse

As his kingdom grew stronger, his spiritual foundation, unfortunately, grew weaker. Like dry rot, pride had slowly eaten it away; and unknown to him, his throne was about to collapse under the weight of his ever-bulging ego.

When he became strong, his heart was so proud that he acted corruptly, and he was unfaithful to the Lord his God, for he entered the temple of the Lord to burn incense on the altar of incense. Then Azariah the priest entered after him and with him eighty priests of the Lord, valiant men. And they opposed Uzziah the king and said to him, "It is not for you, Uzziah, to burn incense to the Lord, but for the priests, the sons of Aaron who are consecrated to burn incense. Get out of the sanctuary, for you have been unfaithful, and will have no honor from the Lord God." But Uzziah, with a censer in his hand for burning incense, was enraged; and while he was enraged with the priests, the leprosy broke out on his forehead before the priests in the house of the Lord, beside the altar of incense. And Azariah the chief priest and all the priests looked at him, and behold, he was leprous on his forehead; and they hurried him out of there, and he himself also hastened to get out because the Lord had smitten him. And King Uzziah was a leper to the day of his death; and he lived in a separate house, being a leper, for he was cut off from the house of the Lord. And Jotham his son was over the king's house judging the people of the land. (vv. 16–21)

What a toll pride takes! Once humble and teachable, Uzziah in his old age had become arrogant, callous, and combative. A spiritual leprosy had secretly been spreading through his soul; now it had broken forth to be visible to all.

Sadder still were the results of his prideful act on his family—particularly his grandson Ahaz. Ahaz's father, Jotham, was twenty-five when his father, Uzziah, vacated the throne. Taking over as king, Jotham ruled sixteen years,

and he did right in the sight of the Lord, according to all that his father Uzziah had done; however he did not enter the temple of the Lord. But the people continued acting corruptly. (27:2)

He wisely modeled his life after Uzziah's earlier years, distinguishing himself as a great civic and military leader (see vv. 3–5). And, having had the image of his father's leprous agony burned into his memory, he did not presumptuously enter the temple. He kept his heart near to God, as the chronicler explains:

Jotham became mighty because he ordered his ways before the Lord his God. (v. 6)

But Jotham's son—and Uzziah's grandson—Ahaz was another story.

Ahaz was twenty years old when he became king, and he reigned sixteen years in Jerusalem; and he did not do right in the sight of the Lord as David his father had done. But he walked in the ways of the kings of Israel; he also made molten images for the Baals. Moreover, he burned incense in the valley of Benhinnom, and burned his sons in fire, according to the abominations of the nations whom the Lord had driven out before the sons of Israel. And he sacrificed and burned incense on the high places, on the hills, and under every green tree. (28:1–4)

With a godly father like Jotham, how could Ahaz have such antipathy toward God? Here's one possible explanation. When Jotham was a boy, Uzziah was seeking the Lord. But when Ahaz was a child, his hero-grandfather Uzziah was in his declining, rebellious years. Perhaps, therefore, Jotham picked up his dad's earlier qualities, while impressionable Ahaz absorbed his grandfather's vices. In other words, when Uzziah sowed the wind, Ahaz reaped the whirlwind.

## Evaluation: Uzziah's Lingering Message

Swirling through time, several lessons from Uzziah's story land at our doorstep. The first is a general warning: *we will never grow too old to sin.* As the years pass, it's tempting to rest on our successes, possessions, and influence, forgetting it is the Lord who has prospered us. Pride can sneak into our unguarded hearts, and before long, we're humming "I did it my way"—and demanding our way with everyone around us. Ask the Lord to help you search your heart to see if a prideful attitude has settled into your spirit.

The second lesson is a twofold message specifically to parents: *you can never measure the positive influence you have on your family, so don't sell it short.* Uzziah made a positive impact on Jotham's life by seeking the Lord and making wise decisions. Just by being yourself, you, too, have great power to affect for good your children, grandchildren, and great-grandchildren—even if you can't fix a bike chain, bait a hook, or build a dollhouse.

Also, *never forget the negative consequences of a rebellious life—don't think you're not being watched.* Remember, your home truly is a museum of memories. Every day, you hang more paintings on the walls. Every moment, you etch another memory into the minds of your Jothams and Ahazes. Does that mean you have to be perfect? No, just faithful to the Lord and humble enough to bow before Him and thank Him for His marvelous help in your life.

According to *Webster's*, an *epitaph* is "a brief statement commemorating or epitomizing a deceased person."[2] Let's isolate Scripture's epitaphs for the four men in the passage we've just studied.

Amaziah:   "He did right in the sight of the Lord, yet not with a whole heart" (2 Chron. 25:2).

Uzziah:   "As long as he sought the Lord, God prospered him. . . . But when he became strong, his heart was so proud that he acted corruptly" (26:5b, 16a).

Jotham:   "Jotham became mighty because he ordered his ways before the Lord his God" (27:6).

Ahaz:   "He did not do right in the sight of the Lord" (28:1b).

As you reflect on the phases of your life, you may see a little of each of these men in yourself. But if you had to choose one that best epitomizes your life now, which would it be, and why?

_____

_____

_____

_____

If your name appeared in Scripture, what epitaph would you want God to write in summing up your life?

_____

_____

_____

_____

So those words can be said of you, what changes, if any, need to occur in your attitudes or behavior?

_____

_____

2. *Webster's Ninth New Collegiate Dictionary*, see "epitaph."

_____

_____

_____

What steps can you take now to begin making those changes?

_____

_____

_____

## 🌹 Living Insights

C. H. Spurgeon had every reason to be proud. He began his pastoral ministry while still a teenager, and by the age of twenty-seven he was

> preaching to crowds of 6,000 in London's Metropolitan Tabernacle, which his congregation had built to accommodate the ever-increasing crowds. . . . [His] sermons were printed in more than twenty languages, including Russian, Chinese, Japanese, and Arabic. . . . American newspapers were printing his sermons in their entirety every week and calling him, "the greatest preacher of the age."[3]

For almost forty years, whenever he preached, thousands thronged to hear him. Like Uzziah, he had fame, power, and influence.

Unlike Uzziah, however, Spurgeon finished his life with his faith intact and his pride in check. As a result, he retained the Lord's blessing and the people's respect.

> Three days after his death, 60,000 mourners came to view his body as it lay in state in the Metropolitan Tabernacle. The funeral service itself had to be given four times to packed congregations. And

_____

3. Tom Carter, comp., *Spurgeon at His Best* (Grand Rapids, Mich.: Baker Book House, 1988), p. 1.

several hundred thousand people lined the streets the entire five miles from the church to Norwood Cemetery, where Spurgeon was buried.[4]

What happened when proud Uzziah died?

> They buried him with his fathers in the field of the grave which belonged to the kings, for they said, "He is a leper." (2 Chron. 26:23b)

Dishonored and cast out, he was remembered not for his great achievements but for his great sin. How can we guard against pride's devastating consequences in our lives? Spurgeon himself offered this observation and advice:

> Pride is like the flies of Egypt; all Pharaoh's soldiers could not keep them out. And I am sure all the strong resolutions and devout aspirations we may have cannot keep pride out unless the Lord God Almighty sends a strong wind of his Holy Spirit to sweep it away.[5]

Right now, release the Spirit to search for any prideful thoughts or attitudes hiding in your heart (see Ps. 139:23–24). As He brings into your mind those swarming bits of vanity, write them down, then ask Him to sweep them out of your heart.

---

---

---

---

---

4. Carter, *Spurgeon at His Best*, p. 2.

5. Carter, *Spurgeon at His Best*, p. 164.

## Chapter 4

# THE PARENTS OF A SON BORN BLIND

*John 9*

Laura's ministry was a surprise to everyone, especially her mother. A mentally retarded child, Laura was usually quiet and withdrawn—until her mother realized that God's words were meant for *all* of His children and began reading her a personalized version of Psalm 23:

> "Jesus is Laura's strong Friend and Protector. He takes care of her in a very special way. Laura cannot see Him but He sees her. She is His darling little lamb."[1]

From that moment, Laura became more vibrant, and a new delight and understanding sparkled in her soft brown eyes. This miraculous change awed her mother and had a tremendous effect on all those near her.

> Her teacher sent a note home: "Laura is so animated; she is singing and telling the other youngsters, 'I love you, kids! I love you!'"
>
> Her speech therapist called: "What are you doing with Laura? She is responsive and bubbly!" My explanation was met with a cautious silence. Then— "If it works, do it. Send the Scripture along, and we'll work on it here too."
>
> This shy, silent, fearful daughter of ours had begun her ministry—to teach me; to exhibit God's power; to bring God's Word into other lives.[2]

That same year around Christmas, Laura's brother, Craig, also mentally retarded, started touching lives in a similar way. He listened closely to his mother's telling of the Nativity story, and soon

---

1. Gloria Hawley, "Gifts of Joy," as quoted by Gene Newman and Joni Eareckson Tada in *All God's Children: Ministry with Disabled Persons*, rev. ed. (Grand Rapids, Mich.: Zondervan Publishing House, 1993), pp. 19–20.

2. Hawley, as quoted by Newman and Tada in *All God's Children*, p. 20.

his teacher called too,

> and, in tears, described how he had told his class about Jesus' birth—the star, God's love, angels and shepherds.
>
> Our little boy, his eyes shining with the light that split the heavens so long ago, spilled over with God's message of unchanging love—to a group of abnormal children no one had thought to tell before.
>
> Craig's ministry had begun.[3]

But this remarkable mother of two extraordinary children gives us a down-to-earth perspective as well as inspiration:

> Craig and Laura remain handicapped. God has not chosen to "heal" them. He is pleased to use them.[4]

God is pleased to use all sorts of disabled people and their families. In fact, the next page of our album overflows with pictures of disabled people God has used. Let's study a few of their portraits to learn about their unique role in God's plan.

## Various Disabilities: A Survey of Scripture

Even if you've studied the Bible for years, you may be surprised at the number of stories focusing on disabled people. In Genesis 27, we find that Abraham's promised son, Isaac, eventually went blind; later, Isaac's son Jacob, after wrestling with an angel, was lame in one leg for the rest of his life (chap. 32). In 2 Samuel 9, there's a touching picture of Mephibosheth, Jonathan's son, who "was lame in both feet" (v. 13b). First Kings 14 shows God using blind Ahijah to prophesy against King Jeroboam. And in 2 Kings 5, we see the Syrian commander Naaman, who had leprosy.

In the New Testament, Jesus encountered disabled people on many occasions—the paralytic whose friends lowered him through the roof (Mark 2); the man with the withered hand (chap. 3); the hearing-impaired man who "spoke with difficulty" (7:32); the two blind men (Matt. 9:27–31); and countless others with all sorts of disabilities and disorders.

Certainly, God places high on His list of useful and capable

---

3. Hawley, as quoted by Newman and Tada in *All God's Children*, p. 20.

4. Hawley, as quoted by Newman and Tada in *All God's Children*, p. 20.

people the handicapped and impaired; we, on the other hand, often overlook them. Even when we read their stories in the Bible, we tend to hurry on to the healing; rarely do we pause to empathize with their suffering.[5] So, as we now turn to examine another family photograph from Scripture, let's step into the picture and experience the story behind the image—the story of the son born blind.

## A Century-One Family: A Son Born Blind

The setting is a busy Jerusalem thoroughfare where Jesus is walking with His disciples. Through the blur of humanity around Him, He fixes His compassionate eyes on a lone beggar, tattered, street-worn, and sightless.

> And as He passed by, He saw a man blind from birth. (John 9:1)[6]

### Physical Handicap

For a moment, imagine the colorlessness of this man's existence. By tightly shutting your eyes, you may be able to experience the darkness, but you still have your store of mental images; you can visualize the golden splendor of a sunrise or the reassurance of your friend's smile. But blackness is all this man has known—smothering, inky blackness. Never has he seen the sun glinting off a glassy lake or the moon glowing in a velvet sky. Not once has he seen the love, or heartbreak, in his parents' eyes. Rather, the choking dust, the noise of people and animals shuffling by, and the occasional clink of a shekel in his cup beat out the monotonous rhythm of his life. But this day, all that would change.

### Spiritual Issue

Sensing some men nearby, the blind man picks up the strands of their conversation:

> And His disciples asked Him, saying, "Rabbi, who sinned, this man or his parents, that he should be born blind?" (v. 2)

5. Empathy is different from sympathy. To sympathize means to feel *for* an individual; to empathize means to feel *with* a person, to enter their world and experience their feelings.

6. "This is the only miracle in the gospels in which the sufferer is said to have been afflicted from his birth." William Barclay, *The Gospel of John*, vol. 2, rev. ed., The Daily Study Bible Series (Philadelphia, Pa.: Westminster Press, 1975), p. 37.

Amateur theologians! They always make the man feel like a freak, a creature behind bars to observe, analyze, but never touch.

We may wonder why the disciples asked such a question. William Barclay explains that, in Jesus' day, Jewish teachers gave two basic reasons for congenital disabilities:

> Some of them had the strange notion of prenatal sin. They actually believed that a man could begin to sin while still in his mother's womb. . . .
>
> The alternative was that the man's affliction was due to the sin of his parents. . . . One of the key-notes of the Old Testament is that the sins of the fathers are always visited upon the children.[7]

So the disciples' question, although insensitive, was logical in light of the prevailing theology. In their minds, the man's blindness was God's punishment; but was it punishment for his sin or his parents' sin?

The blind man waits, dreading the verdict. But the Teacher's answer surprises him:

> "It was neither that this man sinned, nor his parents; but it was in order that the works of God might be displayed in him. We must work the works of Him who sent Me, as long as it is day; night is coming, when no man can work. While I am in the world, I am the light of the world." (vv. 3–5)

Like the disciples, we often see disabled people and frown. "What a pity," we say. "How could this terrible thing have happened?" But God says, "What an opportunity! I'll use this person to show My sensitivity, My power, and My glory." Jesus' response teaches us that disabilities are often the perfect platform upon which the living Lord does His glorious work.

### Supernatural Act

Right away, Jesus follows his statement with action:

> When He had said this, He spat on the ground, and made clay of the spittle, and applied the clay to his eyes, and said to him, "Go, wash in the pool of

---

7. Barclay, *The Gospel of John*, vol. 2, pp. 37–39.

Siloam" (which is translated, Sent). And so he went
away and washed, and came back seeing. (vv. 6–7)

Imagine the man's feelings as the water that washes away the
mud also rinses the black veil of blindness from his eyes. For the
first time, he sees his own hands, the water dripping from them,
the sunlight glistening off the ripples in the pool. As he looks up,
a new world unfolds before him. Color and light cascade through
his mind, flooding his soul with childlike wonder.

### General Reaction

When he returns, word spreads quickly that the blind beggar
can see. But instead of throwing confetti, the people pelt him with
skeptical questions. "Are you really the beggar we used to know?
No, it must be someone who looks like him. It's really you? How
did this happen? Where is this Jesus?" (see vv. 8–12).

Unsure of his story, they take him to the religious police—the
Pharisees (v. 13). Immediately, we are given a sense of their priorities.

> Now it was a Sabbath on the day when Jesus made
> the clay, and opened his eyes. (v. 14)

According to Jewish interpretations of the Mosaic Law, Jesus has
violated the prohibition against working on the Sabbath. So the
Pharisees put the formerly blind man under the interrogator's light,
grilling him with questions. And he just keeps repeating his story:
"He applied clay to my eyes, and I washed, and I see" (v. 15b). See?
It's simple.

However, the spiritually blind Pharisees don't see.

> Some of the Pharisees were saying, "This man [Jesus]
> is not from God, because He does not keep the
> Sabbath." But others were saying, "How can a man
> who is a sinner perform such signs?" And there was
> a division among them. They said therefore to the
> blind man again, "What do you say about Him, since
> He opened your eyes?" And he said, "He is a prophet."
> The Jews therefore did not believe it of him, that he
> had been blind, and had received sight. (vv. 16–18a)

In their minds, the only solution to this enigma is to call the
man a liar. To prove their point, they summon his parents, who
testify that he was born blind. But, intimidated by the powerful

33

Pharisees, who could excommunicate them if they align with Jesus, they plead ignorance about how he was healed (vv. 18b–23). "Ask him," they say. "He is of age, he shall speak for himself" (v. 21b).

> So a second time they called the man who had been blind, and said to him, "Give glory to God; we know that this man is a sinner." He therefore answered, "Whether He is a sinner, I do not know; one thing I do know, that, whereas I was blind, now I see." They said therefore to him, "What did He do to you? How did He open your eyes?" He answered them, "I told you already, and you did not listen; why do you want to hear it again? You do not want to become His disciples too, do you?" And they reviled him, and said, "You are His disciple, but we are disciples of Moses. We know that God has spoken to Moses; but as for this man, we do not know where He is from." The man answered and said to them, "Well, here is an amazing thing, that you do not know where He is from, and yet He opened my eyes. We know that God does not hear sinners; but if anyone is God-fearing, and does His will, He hears him. Since the beginning of time it has never been heard that anyone opened the eyes of a person born blind. If this man were not from God, He could do nothing." They answered and said to him, "You were born entirely in sins, and are you teaching us?" And they put him out. (vv. 24–34)

The Pharisees went to great lengths to disprove this blind man's story. They indicted Jesus' character (v. 24), persistently interrogated the man (v. 26), rebuked him sternly (vv. 28–29), and finally resorted to insult and accusation (v. 34). Still, they couldn't deny his statement: "Whereas I was blind, now I see" (v. 25b). Nor could they deny the inevitable conclusion concerning Jesus: "If this man were not from God, He could do nothing" (v. 33).

So, plugging their ears to the truth, they solve their dilemma by throwing the man out. Case closed.

### Personal Faith

Glad to be free of these hypocrites, yet still confused and disoriented, the man wanders the streets alone. But not for long.

Jesus heard that they had put him out; and finding him, He said, "Do you believe in the Son of Man?" He answered and said, "And who is He, Lord, that I may believe in Him?" Jesus said to him, "You have both seen Him, and He is the one who is talking with you." And he said, "Lord, I believe." And he worshiped Him. (vv. 35–38)

At first, he had seen Jesus only as a man (v. 11); then he saw Him as a prophet (v. 17). But now his spiritual eyes are open, and he sees Jesus as Lord. The light has truly come to this man born in darkness.

## Your Particular Family: A Brief Appraisal

Jesus' encounter with the blind beggar sheds light on a few pertinent principles for everyone. First, *we all struggle with disabilities*. In the story, the blind man wasn't the only person with a disability; the disciples, the neighbors, and the Pharisees were handicapped too. But their disabilities crippled their understanding rather than their bodies—just as that same spiritual infirmity called sin plagues each one of us with its crippling consequences.

Second, *disabilities can destroy or display*. Depending on the choices we make, our disabilities can devastate us with bitterness, anger, or a poor self-image. Or they can be used by God to display His glory—perhaps not through divine healing, but through the kind of ministry little Laura and Craig exemplified.

Third, *physical disabilities provide families an inside channel of spiritual insight*. Certainly, a parent's greatest fear is to have a disabled child. Yet in those who have handicapped children, we often find a rare depth of understanding. Out of the pain, God can forge a mature love that defies pat answers and cold theological ramblings— a compassionate love straight from the heart of Jesus Himself.

## 🌹 *Living Insights*

Joni Eareckson Tada recalls her first experience in church after the tragic diving accident that left her permanently bound to a wheelchair.

There I was, out of the rehab center only a few weeks, sitting upright and awkward in my bulky wheelchair and wondering what to do about Sunday morning. I knew my church had been praying for me since my diving accident two years earlier in 1967, but facing people terrified me. Would they stare? Would I know what to say? Would I have to sit next to my family in the pew, half blocking the middle aisle? And what if I had to wheel into the rest room—would I fit?

What I discovered that Sunday morning, after my family lifted me out of the car and into my wheelchair, changed my entire outlook on church. Someone had hammered together a few pieces of plywood to make a ramp. People smiled and asked me how I was doing at college. Old friends asked me to sit with them and held my Bible and hymnal. The feeling was warm and friendly. I felt welcomed. I belonged.[8]

What if Joni had gone to your church? What obstacles would she have met in her wheelchair? What kind of reception would she have received?

_____

_____

_____

Sometimes we feel awkward around disabled people. What if we say the wrong thing? If they've been severely disfigured, will we find ourselves rudely staring, perhaps uncomfortably looking away? In what ways do you think Jesus' attitude toward the blind beggar can be a model for your attitude toward disabled people? Reread John 9:3–6, 35–38 as you formulate your answer.

_____

_____

_____

In what specific ways can you help disabled people in your

8. Joni Eareckson Tada, in All God's Children, p. 9.

church feel more comfortable when they come to worship?

_____

_____

_____

## 🌹 *Living Insights*

A cerebral palsy victim, Shirley has little control of her muscles. When someone stops to say hello, her face will brighten, but all she can manage is a nod and a wide, welcoming smile. Behind that silent smile, though, is an intelligent, charming person few people take the time to see. One avenue to her inner spirit is the worn book of original poems she always keeps by her side. Peek into the book, and you'll discover Shirley's heart.

### Inside My Heart

Inside my heart, there are feelings that few know
    about.
When people see my wheelchair,
They don't see me as a person,
That I have a mind and a heart.
Once they get to know me,
They see me as a person,
My face shows feeling,
And my eyes tell it all.
My feelings are like a sea—
The water goes up and down,
My life goes up and down, too.
I'm always giving and never taking;
That is the way God wants me to be.
He gave me a heart full of love
For all.[9]

Like Shirley, many disabled people are beautiful displays of God's love. So look past the wheelchairs and braces—get to know the people inside.

---

9. Shirley Fields, "Inside My Heart." Used by permission.

Chapter 5

# A DOUBLE BLESSING FOR A SINGLE PARENT

*1 Kings 17*

Losing a spouse, through either divorce or death, can be like entering a vast wilderness alone. In his book *Single Parenting*, Robert G. Barnes, Jr., describes the experience.

> By far, the most recurring feeling expressed by the "single again" is the loneliness. "As long as I stay busy, doing anything, I'm OK. But when I sit in my bedroom at the end of the day and stare at the walls, I get a knot in my stomach I'm so lonely." This was the way one woman expressed her feelings. . . . The single individual feels that she is groping to find her place in the world around her. Even though people such as friends and family may express their love, a barren feeling still exists inside. The emptiness is so vast it seems to be endless. "How many nights will I wind up in this room crying?"
>
> In this emotional state of mind every challenge in life seems like an attack by a serpent, and the "single again" often feels that she is simply bouncing from the bristles of one cactus to the next. The everyday difficulties—car problems, illness, or disciplining the children—become major hurdles. Just as it is difficult for a traveler to share large amounts of water when he is in a desert, it is also difficult for one who is emotionally drained and thirsty to give continually to those around him.[1]

The prophet Elijah encountered such a parched single parent—the widow of Zarephath. In our album of family pictures, her photograph reveals a painful story of fear and loneliness. How Elijah touched her in her sorrow models a ministry of compassion needed

---

1. Robert G. Barnes, Jr., *Single Parenting: A Wilderness Journey* (Wheaton, Ill.: Tyndale House Publishers, 1988), pp. 15–16.

in our churches. Let's join him prior to their meeting as he is enduring his own wilderness journey.

## When the Brook Dries Up

Elijah has just stepped out of the obscurity of his hometown into the glittering light of King Ahab's throne room. Bravely, he walks up to the wicked king and, pointing a finger in judgment, announces:

> "As the Lord, the God of Israel lives, before whom
> I stand, surely there shall be neither dew nor rain
> these years, except by my word." (1 Kings 17:1b)

Then, in obedience to the Lord's instructions, he escapes into the wilderness.

> The word of the Lord came to him, saying, "Go away
> from here and turn eastward, and hide yourself by
> the brook Cherith, which is east of the Jordan. And
> it shall be that you shall drink of the brook, and I
> have commanded the ravens to provide for you
> there." (vv. 2–4)

With the Lord's promise that He will meet all of Elijah's needs, the prophet flees to the brook Cherith and lives there secure and satisfied, nourished by the cool water and fed by the ravens that "brought him bread and meat in the morning and bread and meat in the evening" (v. 6). But

> it happened after a while, that the brook dried up,
> because there was no rain in the land. (v. 7)

*The brook dried up.* How could this be? Hadn't Elijah said what the Lord told him to say? Hadn't he gone where the Lord told him to go? Hadn't he done what the Lord told him to do? Doubts and fears must have circled his heart like vultures as the flow of life-giving water slowly dwindled until the brook became a dry, peeling riverbed.

This state of confusion was the gall of Elijah's wilderness experience—the bitter liquid tasted by every single parent. What is happening? God provided my spouse for security and nourishment; now I feel so empty and unsure. Where is God? Doesn't He love me?

Perhaps through Elijah's wilderness, God was preparing him to understand the pain he was about to witness. For when the Lord finally speaks again, it is to send him to a certain single parent in Zarephath.

## When the Pain Goes On

> Then the word of the Lord came to him, saying, "Arise, go to Zarephath, which belongs to Sidon, and stay there; behold, I have commanded a widow there to provide for you." So he arose and went to Zarephath, and when he came to the gate of the city, behold, a widow was there gathering sticks. (vv. 8–10a)

### Strange Place

Zarephath means "smelting-place" and comes from a root word meaning "to smelt, refine, test."[2] Indeed, this city has been a place of fire and testing for the widow God tells Elijah to meet. The death of her husband has left her alone to provide for herself and her son in the midst of a severe drought. How will she put food on the table? To whom can she turn for help? For comfort? For companionship?

Identifying with this woman's fear and stress are today's single parents. For them, life also resembles a glowing hot crucible, fired by the daily demands of feeding and clothing a family, making repairs, sorting out the bills. Adding heat is the social awkwardness that single parents must face. Where do they fit in? With married parents? With other singles? Even being around old friends conjures up painful reminders of an inner emptiness and a seemingly unending sense of loss.

For the widow of Zarephath this day, the fire burns even hotter when, unexpectedly, up walks Elijah—another mouth to feed.

### Increased Demands

At first, from her perspective, this man's arrival only increases the demands on her life. Without even a hello, Elijah immediately begins making requests.

> He called to her and said, "Please get me a little water in a jar, that I may drink." And as she was going to

2. William Gesenius, *A Hebrew and English Lexicon of the Old Testament*, trans. Edward Robinson, ed. Francis Brown, S. R. Driver, Charles A. Briggs (Oxford, England: Clarendon Press, n.d.), p. 864.

get it, he called to her and said, "Please bring me a piece of bread in your hand." (vv. 10b–11)

"Get me a little water." "Bring me a piece of bread." Doesn't this poor widow have enough to bear without him adding more weight to her already overwhelming load?

### Limited Resources

But she said, "As the Lord your God lives, I have no bread, only a handful of flour in the bowl and a little oil in the jar; and behold, I am gathering a few sticks that I may go in and prepare for me and my son, that we may eat it and die." (v. 12)

Destitute. Alone. Hopeless. Only death remains as a chilling comforter for this widow and her son.

Then Elijah said to her, "Do not fear; go, do as you have said, but make me a little bread cake from it first, and bring it out to me, and afterward you may make one for yourself and for your son. For thus says the Lord God of Israel, 'The bowl of flour shall not be exhausted, nor shall the jar of oil be empty, until the day that the Lord sends rain on the face of the earth.'" (vv. 13–14)

Opening the thick, black curtains of despair, Elijah's words beam a ray of hope into her heart. Do not fear! Keep guard over your emotions; God will provide; let's act according to His word. Drawing strength from his faith, she risks her only food and obeys.

So she went and did according to the word of Elijah, and she and he and her household ate for many days. The bowl of flour was not exhausted nor did the jar of oil become empty, according to the word of the Lord which He spoke through Elijah. (vv. 15–16)

Imagine the widow's delight each time she looks into the jar of flour. It's full again! And the jar of oil. Full too! Humming praises to the Lord, she stirs the ingredients, stokes the fire, and slips her batter into the oven. Out come these plain, ordinary biscuits, but to her they are a king's feast catered by the Lord Himself.

# When the World Caves In

Soon, though, her laughter turns again to tears. As is often the case with single parents living in the crucible, just when one fire dims, another one flames higher.

### Unexpected Affliction

> Now it came about after these things, that the son of the woman, the mistress of the house, became sick. (v. 17a)

Can you feel the frustration in this verse? After the widow has adjusted to the death of her husband, accepted the harsh realities of raising a son alone, and narrowly escaped starvation; after she has welcomed Elijah into her life and revived her hope in God—suddenly, her precious son becomes ill. His fever rises, the illness intensifies, and once again, death's shadow looms near.

### Impossible Situation

This time, however, there is no escape.

> His sickness was so severe, that there was no breath left in him. (v. 17b)

It can't be! Like Elijah's brook at Cherith, her boy was her life and joy. Now this part of her life has dried up too. And her heart has become broken . . . and bitter.

### Resentful Reaction

Cradling the boy's limp body, she glares at the prophet through her tears:

> "What do I have to do with you, O man of God? You have come to me to bring my iniquity to remembrance, and to put my son to death!" (v. 18)

Graciously, Elijah does not defend himself or God. What answer can one give to a grieving widow holding the lifeless body of her only son? No answer at this moment will suffice, only a tender touch.

> And he said to her, "Give me your son." Then he took him from her bosom and carried him up to the upper room where he was living, and laid him on his own bed. (v. 19)

What can the prophet be thinking? Perhaps he remembers how the Lord fulfilled the prophecy he made to King Ahab and how He later delivered him from the dried-up brook. Maybe he recalls the ravens who brought him food in the wilderness and this recent miracle of flour and oil. Certainly, God can do anything He wills— even resurrect the dead. So he prays,

> "O Lord my God, hast Thou also brought calamity
> to the widow with whom I am staying, by causing
> her son to die?" (v. 20)

Bearing her grief in his heart and countering her despair with his faith, he intercedes for the widow. Then he becomes even more personally involved in her crisis.

> He stretched himself upon the child three times, and
> called to the Lord, and said, "O Lord my God, I pray
> Thee, let this child's life return to him." (v. 21)

Once, twice, three times, Elijah lays on the still body; once, twice, three times, Elijah prays feverishly. Then, miraculously, the boy's finger twitches, an eyelid flutters, and his chest heaves, drawing in a rush of air. He's alive!

> And the Lord heard the voice of Elijah, and the life
> of the child returned to him and he revived. And
> Elijah took the child, and brought him down from
> the upper room into the house and gave him to his
> mother; and Elijah said, "See, your son is alive."
> Then the woman said to Elijah, "Now I know that
> you are a man of God, and that the word of the Lord
> in your mouth is truth." (vv. 22–24)

## When God Comes Through

Wouldn't it be great if God gave that widow's double blessing to every single parent? Imagine having a self-replenishing food pantry and children who never need to see the doctor!

However, God does not always work that way. We cannot promise single parents that their children will grow up healthy and secure; neither can we guarantee that their financial problems will disappear. But we can say that God will be faithful each step of the way through their wilderness journey.

If you are a single parent, be looking for the ways the Lord will exhibit His faithfulness to you. Sometimes He will use another person to meet your need; if so, let Him. Sometimes He will use circumstances; if so, thank Him. And sometimes He will even perform a miracle; if so, believe Him.

For those who aren't single parents, remember Elijah's example of personal ministry. Saying "I'll pray for you" should be just the beginning of a committed involvement in the lives of single parents. Open your heart and your home—provide meals, baby-sit the kids, include their family in your activities, fingerprint your love all over their lives.

You can be their double blessing.

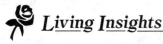 ## Living Insights STUDY ONE

### For Single Parents

As a single parent, you can restore your sense of hope. Life may not become easier—your paycheck may never seem to stretch far enough, your list of chores may never shorten, and your family may never feel quite whole again—but with God's strength, you can build a home for yourself and your children.

How is this possible? A beginning step is to accept the reality of your singlehood, as Robert G. Barnes, Jr., observes,

> One cannot effectively fulfill the role of a nurturing parent until one has dealt with the primary and personal state of being single.[3]

Single parents who have wrapped their identities around their spouses often panic after they're gone. Distressed and insecure, they may unwisely run into the arms of another man or woman or begin relating to their children as substitute spouses. If you accept your singlehood, you may still wrestle with your emotions, but you can also feel confident in the Lord and in the abilities and role He has given you as a single person.

Another step is to help your children realize that a single-parent family is still a family. All children yearn for their absent mom or dad to return. So let your children grieve the loss of your spouse, understanding that they will try to deny the divorce or death, bargain with you or God, feel angry, and even feel guilty that

3. Barnes, *Single Parenting*, p. 15.

somehow they caused your spouse to leave. But in time, help them see that although there is a piece missing in their family circle, they are still part of a close, loving family.

Finally, for your sake and your children's, develop a social network. Admittedly, after a divorce or the death of a spouse, it takes great courage to face people again. You may feel awkward around married couples and out of place in a singles' group. But don't let guilt, embarrassment, or fear surround you with walls of isolation that only reinforce your loneliness. If invitations are slow in coming, take the initiative and invite others into your home. In fact, won't you take out your calendar right now and schedule some social times for your family this month?

Breaking down the barrier of isolation, helping your family feel like a family, and making your house feel like a home may be the hardest tasks you've ever faced. But when the job seems impossible, cling to the Lord's promise to you as a single parent:

> A father of the fatherless and a judge for the
>   widows,
> Is God in His holy habitation.
> God makes a home for the lonely.
> (Ps. 68:5–6a)

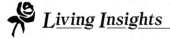

## Living Insights

### For Friends of Single Parents

Bill [my husband] had dropped out of church about five years before he was killed. As a widow, I attended church for seven more years before I was invited to another Christian's home—a total of twelve years.

I spent the first nine of those years in my home church. I often invited couples and small groups of married people to my home for meals, hosted church parties, and invited single ladies to lunch. But never once in that time did the children and I receive an invitation in return.[4]

4. Elizabeth Baker, *Wanting to Follow, Forced to Lead* (Wheaton, Ill.: Tyndale House Publishers, 1991), pp. 92–93.

Does this woman's story sadden you? Is her experience true of single-parent families in your church?

Elijah modeled a personal ministry with the widow of Zarephath and her son. The following list gives some ways you, too, can reach out to single-parent families in your church or neighborhood. Pick an idea you like, or let this list spark your creativity to come up with ideas of your own. But do make plans to put them into action soon.

✓ Offer free baby-sitting.

✓ Volunteer to take care of the yard work.

✓ Find out what's broken and fix it.

✓ Build a go-cart with the kids.

✓ Call once a week.

✓ Pay for the children's music lessons.

✓ Extend a dinner invitation.

✓ Carpool together to church.

✓ Keep the kids after school.

✓ Take the kids to an amusement park.

✓ _____

✓ _____

✓ _____

✓ _____

✓ _____

✓ _____

✓ _____

Chapter 6

# EARNING THE RIGHT TO BE CALLED "DAD"
### Luke 15:11–32

Would you like to hold her?"

His trance broken, he saw the nurse smiling at him—a new father who had been gazing raptly at his daughter, now only one hour old.

The nurse bundled the baby, then lifted her to him. "Support her head . . . like this," she said.

As she placed the sleeping newborn in his arms, a heavy weight called fatherhood settled on his shoulders. Looking at the child's delicate face, he thought of her innocence. What did she know of the world and its dangers? Of the greed and the violence and the darkness? It was up to him, now, to protect and nurture her—this flower so fragile.

Most fathers can recall the moment they first sensed fatherhood's weight of responsibility, as well as the overwhelming feeling of inadequacy. To you, we say, "Be encouraged." The photograph we'll describe on this page of our family album is of a dad who models many qualities of a good father—qualities you can emulate.

You'll find that his example is quite different from many of the models we see today, perhaps even the one you grew up with. To help chart your course in this father's direction, let's begin by first examining some of the pitfalls to avoid. Once these are successfully skirted, you'll be well on your way to earning the right to be called "Dad."

## Familiar Fathers: A Negative Glance

The first type of man who stumbles under fatherhood's load is the *irresponsible dad*. This father tends to slough off the weight with empty promises and chronic procrastination. "I'll get to that" is often his favorite phrase. "The children need your attention"— "OK, I'll get to that." "Your son's bike needs repairing"—"Yeah, I'll get to that." "The finances are out of control"—"Right, I'll get to that. Soon, I promise." The trouble is, he never does.

Then there's the *negative dad*. He is the Captain Ahab of dads—irritable, impatient, and inflexible. Rules must be followed with blind obedience, and keelhauling awaits any child who steps out of line.

The *absent dad* is the third type. This man is a stranger in his own home. He may be present, somewhere behind the newspaper, but he is not there emotionally. His world is his workplace. At home, family life whirls by while he minds his own business—distant and preoccupied.

Finally, faster than a speeding teenager, more powerful than a defiant two-year-old, able to leap tall dilemmas in a single bound . . . it's *Super Dad!* Tim Hansel describes this type of father:

> Super Dad never gets ruffled. Super Dad always has
> the answers. Super Dad is in control. He directs and
> orchestrates—and sometimes, I suppose, he dictates
> with polish and aplomb.[1]

Have you caught yourself trying to be Super Dad? Or wishing you could be absent? Or realizing you're too negative? Or wanting to slough off responsibility? These are ways we cope with the pressures of fatherhood. But we don't have to resort to these roles; we can choose another model to follow—the father Jesus described in his parable of the prodigal son.

## One Father: A Positive Study

You're probably familiar with the foolish prodigal son in this story: how he spent his inheritance on riotous living; then, after the money ran out, he repentantly returned home. But what about the father? What do we know about him? And what can we deduce about his character?

### His Family and Lifestyle

Jesus began the parable, "A certain man had two sons" (Luke 15:11) —two adult sons, as the story soon reveals. We know the father was affluent, for when the younger son asked for his share of the "estate," his father "divided his *wealth* between them" (v. 12, emphasis added). Also, the father had servants (vv. 17, 22, 26), owned nice clothing and jewelry (v. 22), and bred cattle (v. 23).

---

1. Tim Hansel, *What Kids Need Most in a Dad* (Old Tappan, N.J.: Fleming H. Revell Co., 1984), pp. 34–35.

In order to have become so wealthy, the father was probably a wise, responsible, hardworking manager of the family business. We say "family" business because his sons worked for him. And from the older son's comment later in verse 29, we can draw some conclusions about his leadership ability in that he gave the commands, showing that he was actively in charge.

Indeed, the father held the reins in the family, but how well did he relate to his children?

### His Relationship with the Younger Son

As we focus on his relationship with his younger son, the prodigal, several qualities come into view. Apparently, *he had cultivated an honest and open environment*, for the son said boldly, "Father, give me the share of the estate that falls to me" (v. 12a). He felt free to approach his dad with this potentially volatile request. Had there been no openness in their relationship, imagine the imbroglio that could have ensued:

"You want what?"

"My money—now."

"Nothing doing. You'll just throw it away."

"I'm of age. It's mine. I want it."

"Do your chores, and quit bothering me with this nonsense."

"You're so . . . unreasonable!"

"I can be unreasonable—I'm your father. Now get back to work!"

Instead of arguing with his son, though, this dad patiently listened. When the time came to respond to his son's words, this father revealed another aspect of their relationship: it was *mature and secure*.

> "And he divided his wealth between them. And not many days later, the younger son gathered everything together and went on a journey into a distant country, and there he squandered his estate with loose living." (vv. 12b–13)

A less secure man might have clung to his wealth and power, but notice that this father apportioned the inheritance not only to

49

the younger son but also to the elder. He divided the estate, which, according to A. T. Robertson, is "an old and common verb to part in two, cut asunder."[2] Placing all his holdings on the table, he gave each son his cut of the money.[3]

It required a high level of maturity for the father to trust his sons in this way. It also implied a vulnerability on his part and a willingness to give sacrificially—qualities of genuine love that the prodigal would not forget when his new cruise ship lifestyle suddenly sprang a leak.

> "Now when he had spent everything, a severe famine occurred in that country, and he began to be in need. And he went and attached himself to one of the citizens of that country, and he sent him into his fields to feed swine. And he was longing to fill his stomach with the pods that the swine were eating, and no one was giving anything to him. But when he came to his senses, he said, 'How many of my father's hired men have more than enough bread, but I am dying here with hunger! I will get up and go to my father, and will say to him, "Father, I have sinned against heaven, and in your sight; I am no longer worthy to be called your son; make me as one of your hired men."'" (vv. 14–19)

While all this was happening, the father knew nothing. Because he deeply loved his son, this period of silence must have been agonizing. But we don't read of any panic, loss of sleep, or bitterness. He didn't send out a search party or second-guess himself into paralyzing guilt. Instead, expressing another quality of fatherhood, *he calmly and confidently waited*. How difficult that is for any dad! Yet, he stepped back and allowed room for God to work in the young man's life.

When the boy does come to his senses in the pigsty, notice how his thoughts shed light on his relationship with his dad.

---

2. Archibald Thomas Robertson, *Word Pictures in the New Testament* (Grand Rapids, Mich.: Baker Book House, 1930), vol. 2, p. 208.

3. According to Deuteronomy 21:17, the older son would have received a double portion—in this case, two-thirds of the estate; and the younger, one-third.

- "I will get up and go to my father"—his focus was on his father, not just on going home.

- "I have sinned"—he remembered his father's theology and, perhaps through his father's example, had learned how to admit wrong and apologize.

- "I am no longer worthy"—he didn't blame his father or brother for his decision. So, with muck still caking his bare feet and the stench of squalor clinging to his tattered clothes, "he got up and came to his father" (v. 20a).

His father. Though calm and confident, he certainly wasn't passive. Most likely, he had been checking the horizon every morning in hopes of seeing the familiar figure of his boy. Then one day, far down the dirt road, came a lone man, lean and shabby. Squinting through the sun and dust, the father stopped his work and peered into the distance. Could it be? The man resembled his boy, but look at his rags, his matted hair, his sun-blistered skin.

It was his son! Dropping what was in his hands, he instinctively started to run. His sandals slapped the hard dirt road as he rushed to him. Wrapping his arms around him, he welcomed home his lost boy with a thousand kisses (v. 20).

This scene reveals an additional quality about the father: *he modeled authentic Christianity.* He overflowed with Christlike love and forgiveness. And further exhibiting our Lord's grace and mercy, he began heaping gifts and privileges upon the prodigal before he could even finish his repentance speech.

> "And the son said to him, 'Father, I have sinned against heaven and in your sight; I am no longer worthy to be called your son.' But the father said to his slaves, 'Quickly bring out the best robe and put it on him, and put a ring on his hand and sandals on his feet; and bring the fattened calf, kill it, and let us eat and be merry; for this son of mine was dead, and has come to life again; he was lost, and has been found.' And they began to be merry." (vv. 21–24)

Celebration time! However, there was one person who wasn't too eager to celebrate.

### His Relationship with the Older Son

Not only does the father's interaction with his younger boy enlighten us about his character, but so do his dealings with his elder son. When the older boy returned to the house from working in the fields, he wondered what the music and dancing was all about. When he discovered the reason, "he became angry, and was not willing to go in" (v. 28a). Graciously, his father takes the initiative to go out to him. But this son is too mad to listen to his father's entreaties.

> "'Look! For so many years I have been serving you, and I have never neglected a command of yours; and yet you have never given me a kid, that I might be merry with my friends; but when this son of yours came, who had devoured your wealth with harlots, you killed the fattened calf for him.'" (vv. 29–30)

In the father's response, notice this quality of a good dad: *he turns a would-be argument into affirmation.*

> "'My child, you have always been with me, and all that is mine is yours.'" (v. 31)

Then he exhibits another attribute: *he helps his son focus on his brother's present repentance rather than on his previous rebellion.*

> "'We had to be merry and rejoice, for this brother of yours was dead and has begun to live, and was lost and has been found.'" (v. 32)

We have much to learn about maturity and love from this father, don't we? As we step away from the story, how can we package these principles to carry with us?

## All Fathers Who "Earn the Right": An Affirming Word

Most of us would agree that children are easily impressionable, always growing, and emotionally fragile. The father in our story also seemed to recognize this. So let's look at some general principles from his example that we can use in meeting our children's needs.

First, since children are impressionable, they need *credibility*. Fathers must represent in the home what they affirm in church; in other words, they need to resist hypocrisy.

Second, since children are continually growing and maturing, they need room—they need *freedom*. Fathers must remember that God is working in their children in ways they cannot. In other words, dads need to give their children room to fail and grow.

Third, since children are emotionally fragile, they need *under-standing*. Fathers must refuse to let personal struggles harm their children's security and growth. In other words, dads need to take the time and energy to know their children and to help their children know and like themselves.

Remember—at the moment of his baby's birth, a man receives the title *father*, but his love and commitment earn him the right to be called "Dad."

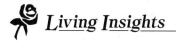 **Living Insights**

### For Dads

When do you recall first feeling the weight of fatherhood on your shoulders?

_____

_____

_____

_____

_____

How have you been holding up under the load? Have you stumbled now and again? Don't worry, all fathers do. In fact, the first step toward building enough strength to carry the weight is admitting your stumblings.

Why don't you talk to your wife about the load you carry and the way you view yourself as a father? You'll be amazed how much that openness will enhance your relationships at home. Here's a way to begin, if you feel at a loss for words.

- Read to your wife what you just wrote about the first time you felt the weight of fatherhood.

- Express what it feels like to be responsible for the family.

- Admit to her times you've caught yourself trying to be Super Dad or wishing you could be absent or realizing you're too negative or wanting to slough off responsibility.

- With your wife, choose one quality exhibited by the prodigal son's dad and make it a goal for yourself.

- Discuss with her how you can accomplish this goal. This week, take a step toward that goal by choosing one new action. In the months ahead, continue improving your fathering skills, one step at a time.[4]

### For Moms

Your job, moms? Encourage, encourage, encourage. You can help your husband succeed as a father by noticing all the positive parenting skills he already possesses. Here are a few samples of encouraging words you can use to bolster his confidence:

- "Did you see how Junior beamed when you complimented him?"

- "Our daughters are fortunate to have you as their dad."

- "The kids always look forward to your coming home from work."

- "The children have never had so much fun as when you wrestled with them the other night."

- "We need you."

### 🌹 Living Insights

### For Sons and Daughters

Perhaps you can identify with Moss Hart's recollection of a day he saw his father as more than his dad, as a person with hopes and struggles too.

> We hurried on, our heads bent against the wind,
> to the cluster of lights ahead that was 149th Street
> and Westchester Avenue, and those lights seemed

4. To help you further examine your fathering style and skills, the National Center for Fathering (217 Southwind Place, Manhattan, KS 66502) has developed a Personal Fathering Profile kit. We recommend that you contact them for information about this and other resources, as well as possible seminars in your area.

to me the brightest lights I had ever seen. Tugging at my father's coat, I started down the line of pushcarts. . . . I would merely pause before a push-cart to say, with as much control as I could muster, "Look at that chemistry set!" or, "There's a stamp album!" or, "Look at the printing press!" Each time my father would pause and ask the pushcart man the price. Then without a word we would move on to the next pushcart. Once or twice he would pick up a toy of some kind and look at it and then at me, as if to suggest this might be something I might like, but I was ten years old and a good deal beyond just a toy; my heart was set on a chemistry set or a printing press. There they were on every pushcart we stopped at, but the price was always the same and soon I looked up and saw we were nearing the end of the line. Only two or three more pushcarts remained. My father looked up, too, and I heard him jingle some coins in his pocket. In a flash I knew it all. He'd gotten together about seventy-five cents to buy me a Christmas present, and he hadn't dared say so in case there was nothing to be had for so small a sum. As I looked up at him I saw a look of despair and disappointment in his eyes that brought me closer to him than I had ever been in my life. I wanted to throw my arms around him and say, "It doesn't matter. . . . I understand. . . . This is better than a chemistry set or a printing press. . . . I love you." But instead we stood shivering beside each other for a moment—then turned away from the last two pushcarts and started silently back home. . . . I didn't even take his hand on the way home nor did he take mine. We were not on that basis. Nor did I ever tell him how close to him I felt that night—that for a little while the concrete wall between father and son had crumbled away and I knew that we were two lonely people struggling to reach each other.[5]

5. Moss Hart, as quoted by Robert A. Raines in *Creative Brooding* (Toronto, Canada: Macmillan Co., Collier-Macmillan, 1966), pp. 45–46.

Can you remember the first time you knew your father as a person and not just as your dad? What were the circumstances? How did you feel?

_____

_____

_____

_____

_____

_____

_____

Were you able to take his hand, or did a wall silently crumble with no one acknowledging it?

_____

_____

_____

_____

If it is possible, talk to your father soon, throw your arms around him, and let him know you love him—imperfections and all.

## Chapter 7

# FROM CAPTIVE TO QUEEN: AN ADOPTION STORY

### The Book of Esther

Pregnant. Unwed. Alone.

Three simple words describe the complex dilemma facing thousands of young women this very moment. What should they do? One woman has described in agonizing terms the decision many women make . . . and the rationale.

> What will I do? Splashing water on my face, wishing this was all a nightmare, I cry. Something is growing in me, infesting me, and wrecking my life. This is not happening! I've got to do something fast to get rid of this infested guilt. It's a simple procedure. It will hurt, but it won't hurt as bad as reality. I will escape this yet!
>
> Ahhhhh!! What am I doing? I'm fixing a big mistake. Yes, that's it. I'm just fixing something. No one has to know.[1]

For many women who feel caged in by an unplanned pregnancy, abortion appears to be the only escape. But adopted fourteen-year-old Jason has a different perspective:

> Once when I was a lot younger I watched a television show on abortion. I saw how many thousands of women were aborting their babies. . . . I remember how glad I was that my biological mother chose

---

This chapter has been adapted from the lesson "From Captive to Queen: An Adoption Story," in the study guide *Old Testament Characters*, rev. ed., coauthored by Ken Gire, from the Bible-teaching ministry of Charles R. Swindoll (Fullerton, Calif.: Insight for Living, 1991), pp. 68–74.

1. Terri West, "Abortion in the United States," (Paper for Law and Religion seminar, Seaver College, Pepperdine University, London Program, Spring 1989), as quoted by F. LaGard Smith in *When Choice Becomes God* (Eugene, Oreg.: Harvest House Publishers, 1990), p. 187.

to carry me and my twin brother Josh to full term and give birth. Then she let us be adopted into a wonderful family. I might not even be here today, except that my biological mother loved me enough to let me be born. And my new family loved me enough to make a wonderful home for me.[2]

Jason's birth mother confronted the same dilemma as the millions of young women who have chosen to abort . . . yet she chose life, while sadly, the others chose death.

This lesson is about those who choose life. We want to celebrate the Jasons in the world and all their courageous birth mothers and adoptive parents. In so doing, we enthusiastically affirm adoption as an answer not only for the woman facing an unplanned pregnancy but for the childless couple and the parentless child as well.

In fact, a certain adopted orphan's photograph fills the next page of our family album. Her name is Esther. Surprised? Yes, the bejeweled Queen Esther was once an orphan, and her story is a sparkling testimonial to the wonder of adoption.

## The Theology of Adoption

Adoption is an ancient practice, dating back at least to the time when Pharaoh's daughter found Moses floating in a basket on the Nile. The Scriptures dress adoption in theological garb, specifically when Paul refers to it in Romans 8—his *magnum opus* about life in the family of God. Let's take a moment to look at some of the benefits of being adopted into His family.

First, we are protected forever from God's condemnation (v. 1). Second, we are set free from the oppressive bondage of sin and death (v. 2). Third, we receive the Holy Spirit, who empowers us to spurn the flesh (v. 4). Fourth, we gain a mind-set of life and peace (v. 6). Fifth, we have the righteousness of God (v. 10). Sixth, we have assurance that we will be resurrected from the dead (v. 11).

Galatians 4 underscores these rich truths about adoption:

> God sent forth His Son, born of a woman, born under the Law, in order that He might redeem those who were under the Law, that we might receive the

---

2. Jason Eisenman, as quoted by Ron Lee Davis with James D. Denney in *Mistreated* (Portland, Oreg.: Multnomah Press, 1989), p. 137.

58

adoption as sons. (vv. 4b–5)[3]

In other words, God reaches into the slave market of sin, breaks our fetters, and redeems us as we come to Him by faith.[4] We are no longer slaves, but children and heirs through God (v. 7).

Strangely, many of us who have accepted God's offer of salvation are still trying to find a way to repay Him. We come to Him with one hand extended and the other groping around in our front pocket for loose change. It's our instinct to want to pay our own way—after all, we've got to be responsible.

Have you let the "if anyone will not work, neither let him eat" principle infect your theology?[5] Do you think that the more church committees you belong to, Sunday school classes you teach, Third World children you sponsor, the more worthy you'll be of God's gift of eternal life?

The gift did come at a great price—God's only begotten Son. But to us, it comes free—without strings or buy-now, pay-later conditions. It's been paid for, totally, by Jesus.

## A Biography of Adoption

The book of Esther illustrates the theological truth of adoption biographically. Esther was a young Jewish orphan who was mercifully adopted by her cousin Mordecai (2:5–7). Her drama stars three more characters: Ahasuerus, king of Persia; Vashti, the king's beautiful wife; and Haman, the hissable villain. Interestingly, the book of Esther is the only one in the Bible that doesn't mention the name of God. But even though His name is absent, His providential fingerprints can be found throughout.[6] Replete with action and intrigue, this ancient story of adoption still speaks to us today.

---

3. The term *adoption* comes from a combination of two Greek words: *huios*, meaning "son," and *tithēmi*, which means "to place, lay, or set." The result is the term *huiothesia*, which means "the placement of a son." See also Romans 9:4 and Ephesians 1:5.

4. The Greek word for *redemption* is used of the price to redeem something that is in pawn, to ransom prisoners of war, or to buy a slave's freedom. Titus 2:13b–14 lists the price of our salvation: "our great God and Savior, Christ Jesus; who gave *Himself* for us" (emphasis added; see also Mark 10:45; 1 Tim. 2:6; Rom. 3:24).

5. 2 Thessalonians 3:10b.

6. Too often, if God's name isn't billboarded in front of us, we can't sense His closeness. But He doesn't always advertise His presence; sometimes He only whispers it, wanting us to be sensitive to His subtle ways. Just as Adam and Eve heard the sound of God walking in the garden (Gen. 3:8), we also need to listen for His unmistakable footsteps as He sovereignly walks the earth.

### A Feast Marked by Punishment

The story opens as King Ahasuerus is throwing a big bash for the entire populace of Susa, the capital city of the Persian Empire (1:5). During the seven days of this revelry, "the royal wine was plentiful according to the king's bounty" (v. 7). On the seventh day, when "the king was merry with wine," he sends for Queen Vashti to come and parade her beauty in front of his guests (vv. 10–11).

But Vashti says no, which in her day was not a popular thing to do. Many modern women would applaud her self-respecting conduct, but not King Ahasuerus. His wrath burns so fiercely that he seeks counsel on what disciplinary measures he should take with her (vv. 12–15). Concerned that the queen's actions will license other Persian wives to disobey their husbands, the king's advisors recommend that he ban her from his presence and replace her with a more deserving woman (vv. 16–22).

### An Ancient Beauty Contest

To find Vashti's replacement, the king stages a beauty pageant. The entire kingdom is scoured so he can choose the most beautiful young virgin. Mordecai enters Esther in the contest, advising her not to reveal her Jewish background. And as the finger of God begins to move through the streets of Susa, it lands sovereignly on Esther.

> And the king loved Esther more than all the women,
> and she found favor and kindness with him more than
> all the virgins, so that he set the royal crown on her
> head and made her queen instead of Vashti. (2:17)

### A Crucial Subplot

After this climactic scene, the story wanders to a seemingly extraneous subplot. Mordecai learns of a plot to assassinate the king and reports it to Esther, who then informs the king "in Mordecai's name" (v. 22). After a thorough investigation, Mordecai's information is verified, the two conspirators are hanged, and it is "written in the Book of the Chronicles in the king's presence" (v. 23). Tuck this away in your mind until later. After seeing more of God's sovereign hand, we will understand this scene's significance.

### A Promotion and a Plot

Meanwhile, Haman is promoted to the king's right-hand man, and the king commands everyone to pay homage to him (3:1–2a).

Mordecai, however, aware of Haman's greed and conceit, "neither bowed down nor paid homage" (v. 2b)—an act of disobedience he was not about to get away with.

> When Haman saw that Mordecai neither bowed down nor paid homage to him, Haman was filled with rage. But he disdained to lay hands on Mordecai alone, for they had told him who the people of Mordecai were; therefore Haman *sought to destroy all the Jews*, the people of Mordecai, who were throughout the whole kingdom of Ahasuerus. (vv. 5–6, emphasis added)

An ancient holocaust takes shape in the mind of this Old Testament Hitler. Gaining the ear of the king, Haman snivels out a story of a "certain people" in his kingdom who "do not observe the king's laws, so it is not in the king's interest to let them remain" (v. 8). In short, Haman offers to pay ten thousand silver talents—which will ultimately find their way to the king's treasuries—to anyone who will help destroy these "different" people (v. 9).

"What?!" the king must be thinking. "Someone else in my kingdom dares to disobey my word? I showed Vashti and I'll show them." And with that, he falls right into Haman's insidious designs and hands the people over, "to do with them as you please" (vv. 10–11).

### A Creative Plan

After discovering Haman's plot, Mordecai and all the Jewish people mourn (4:1–3). When Esther hears of the plot, she inquires about the details but stops short of offering any real help (vv. 4–12). Mordecai then sends this convicting word by way of a messenger:

> "Do not imagine that you in the king's palace can escape any more than all the Jews. For if you remain silent at this time, relief and deliverance will arise for the Jews from another place and you and your father's house will perish. And who knows whether you have not attained royalty for such a time as this?" (vv. 13–14)

It's as if Mordecai is saying, "This is your meeting with destiny, Esther. This is why God had me take you in as a little girl and rear you His way. Don't be silent. Speak up!" And Esther gives this reply:

> "Go, assemble all the Jews who are found in Susa,

and fast for me; do not eat or drink for three days, night or day. I and my maidens also will fast in the same way. And thus I will go in to the king, which is not according to the law; and if I perish, I perish." (v. 16)

Risking her life, Esther comes before the king without a summons. He welcomes her into his presence and beckons her to make her request. Working her way up to it, she first invites him and Haman to a banquet she has prepared. While they dine, she invites them to a second banquet on the following day, when she promises to reveal her petition (5:1–8).

His head swelling at having hobnobbed with royalty, Haman leaves the feast walking on air. But he instantly deflates at the sight of Mordecai, who still refuses to bow down to him. Enraged, Haman orders a gallows built and plots to have Mordecai hanged the next morning (vv. 9–14).

### A Reading of Remembrance and Overdue Honor

That night, to the lullaby of hammer blows, Haman sleeps soundly. King Ahasuerus, however, does not, so he gives "an order to bring the book of records, the chronicles, and they were read before the king" (6:1). Reminded that Mordecai had tipped him off about the assassination conspiracy, King Ahasuerus realizes he has never been rewarded. So the king sends for Haman and asks, "What is to be done for the man whom the king desires to honor?" (v. 6).

Certain that the king wants to honor *him*, Haman goes for the very best: this person should wear one of the king's robes, one of his crowns, and ride one of his horses, while being paraded through the city square by one of the king's most noble princes (vv. 7–9).

Taking his advice, the king orders Haman to do just that—for Mordecai! After carrying out the king's wishes, the horrified Haman "hurried home, mourning, with his head covered" (v. 12b). His days are numbered, and he knows it (v. 13).

### Exposure and Justice

With hardly time to catch his breath, Haman is summoned to Esther's banquet (v. 14). The king again asks her to reveal her request, and now Esther senses that the moment is right.

"If I have found favor in your sight, O king, and if it please the king, let my life be given me as my petition, and my people as my request; for we have been sold, I and my people, to be destroyed, to be killed and to be annihilated. Now if we had only been sold as slaves, men and women, I would have remained silent, for the trouble would not be commensurate with the annoyance to the king." (7:3–4)

Outraged at this affront to his queen, Ahasuerus demands, "Who is he, and where is he, who would presume to do thus?" (v. 5). Esther responds, "A foe and an enemy, is this wicked Haman!" (v. 6). And with swift, ironic retribution, the terrified Haman is hanged on the very gallows he had built to execute Mordecai.

Haman's plot to destroy the Jews is foiled because of Esther— an adopted woman who courageously risked her life to save her people. The book closes with the Feast of Purim, which is still celebrated by Jews around the world in Esther's honor (8:1–10:3).

## The Practicality of Adoption

Esther's story illustrates the beauty of spiritual adoption as well as physical adoption. Remembering the following three truths will help us see the unique significance of adoption.

First: *The adoption process best models the way people enter God's family.* Families with adopted children are living illustrations of salvation. Like adoptive parents, who reach into humanity and *choose* a child—and not on the child's merit—God has mercifully reached out and said, "I choose you for My own."

Second: *Adopted children often become God's special instruments.* Their destinies have been changed; many have been preserved, rescued from dire circumstances to fulfill God's purposes in the light of His love.

Third: *People who are touched by the adopted realize how profound God's plan is.* If you've known adopted children, you understand the graciousness of God's redemptive design.

With hindsight, we can see God's hand in each detail of Esther's story. Separately, the details are like scattered pearls. But God took these pearls, strung them together, and added a clasp to create something beautiful and useful.

Like the destiny of an adopted child—who was not aborted but allowed to live—our destinies were altered when we became part of God's family. The individual pearls of our lives have been threaded together to form a life of purpose and meaning. We have been saved from the death we were headed for and have been chosen instead to live.

## 🌹 Living Insights

You may be struggling with one of the toughest choices of your life. Although you're a Christian, you're pregnant out of wedlock or your girlfriend is pregnant or someone dear to you is in this troubling situation. Or perhaps you are married but just can't see how you can possibly afford yet another mouth to feed.

You may feel panicked, ashamed, torn up inside, desperate. Desperate enough to do *anything* to make this problem just go away.

May we come close and put an arm around you for the next few moments? Not to preach, not to condemn—just to draw near and talk with you.

Many people today would have you believe that abortion is your most sensible way out: it's quick, it's secret, and, besides, it's legal. What they obscure from your view, though, is that it's painful, it's not always safe, and it's a choice for death. Not only your baby's, but yours as well. It's the death of your dreams, of a piece of your heart. It will taint your memories always, and instead of freeing you to resume your life, it will lock you in a pattern of dissociating from this part of yourself.

Doesn't seem so sensible when you really look at it, does it? But what else can you do?

How about considering adoption? It's not easy, by any means; it's not quick; and it's certainly not secret. But it is a choice for life—your baby's as well as yours.

In her booklet *A Case for Adoption*, Cheryl Kreykes Brandsen urges those who counsel people at such a crossroads to

> assist birthparents in recognizing the feelings of care and concern they have for their unborn children. . . . Allowing a child to be born is certainly one of the greatest expressions of love a birthparent can give during a time when it is so convenient to dispose of one's "mistake." . . . Many birthparents acknowledge, often with embarrassment, that when they are alone, they talk to their children about their pregnancies, their plans to release, and their hopes

and fears regarding this. It is important for birth-parents to recognize that these acts of protecting, nourishing, and nurturing their unborn children are deeds of love. It is also important that birthparents see adoption as a response to strong maternal instinct just as surely as parenting is. Most birthmothers who release love their children in a self-sacrificing way. Their love is so great that the needs and best interests of their children are considered primary.[7]

Releasing your child to the arms of another will rend your heart, and we don't make light of that. But love will be doing the rending, not guilt, not death. Won't you consider this option, for the good of your baby . . . and yourself?

For clear information about the adoption process, we encourage you to read the following sources:

A Loving Choice. Grand Rapids, Mich.: Bethany Productions, 1990.

Lindsay, Jeanne Warren. Open Adoption: A Caring Option. Buena Park, Calif.: Morning Glory Press, 1987.

————. Parents, Pregnant Teens and the Adoption Option: Help for Families. Buena Park, Calif.: Morning Glory Press, 1989.

————. Pregnant Too Soon: Adoption Is an Option. Rev. ed. Buena Park, Calif.: Morning Glory Press, 1988.

Lindsay, Jeanne Warren, and Catherine Paschal Monserrat. Adoption Awareness: A Guide for Teachers, Counselors, Nurses and Caring Others. Buena Park, Calif.: Morning Glory Press, 1989.

VanDerMolen, Henrietta. Pregnant and Alone: How You Can Help an Unwed Friend. Wheaton, Ill.: Harold Shaw Publishers, 1989.

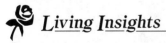 Living Insights                                              STUDY TWO

Adoption is challenging not only for the birth mother but also for the prospective adoptive parents. What will it be like, they wonder. Will we be able to raise an adopted child successfully?

7. Cheryl Kreykes Brandsen, A Case for Adoption (Grand Rapids, Mich.: Bethany Christian Services, 1985), pp. 16–17.

Cheryl Kreykes Brandsen offers encouraging words.

> While parents who have adopted will not expe-
> rience more problems than biological parents be-
> cause of the adoption, they will be faced with
> different parenting tasks. They must tell their child
> that he/she is adopted, and they must help him/her
> form a positive self-image and identity based on dual
> heritage. Openness, honesty, and a sensitivity to the
> feelings each has are essential in this process. . . .
> Adoptive parents who are comfortable with adop-
> tion and with their child's different heritage will
> likely have well-adjusted children.[8]

That's good news! With some wise counsel and lots of love, you
can raise stable, healthy adopted children. The "love" part is up to
you, but here are a couple of resources for finding some counsel:
Bethany Christian Services, 901 Eastern Avenue, NE, Grand Rapids, Michigan 49503, (616) 459-6273; and *The Whole Life Adoption
Book* by Jayne E. Schooler (Colorado Springs, Colo.: NavPress,
1993).

---

8. Brandsen, A *Case for Adoption*, p. 25.

## Chapter 8

# IF YOU HAVE THE SOLO . . . SING OUT!

### 1 Corinthians 7:6–9, 25–35

In a few moments, the curtain would rise. The metal chairs in the school cafeteria clanked and clattered as the parents and assorted relatives bumped their way to their seats, chatting noisily. Backstage, five-year-old Carl—in his rabbit costume—shifted from foot to foot, rehearsing his four-line solo:

> I'm a little bunny, hop hop hop.
> My ears are long and funny, hop hop hop.
> I wiggle my nose when you tickle my toes,
> 'Cause I'm a little bunny, hop hop hop.

He gulped hard and sang it to himself again. Why did he have to be the rabbit? His friend, Warren, got to be the bee; all he had to do was run around the stage and say "Buzzzz"! Carl adjusted his glasses and peeked around the curtain. Sitting there were his older sister Ruthie, Mommy and Daddy, Aunt Jamie . . . and *all those people!* He felt queasy.

"Carl," Mrs. Tate whispered hoarsely, "are we in our places?"

Ears drooping, Carl moved over behind Lorraine, the petunia. Suddenly, the rumbling din on the other side of the curtain quieted, and Mr. Gonce, the principal, welcomed everyone. Finally he announced: "Now . . . 'A Day in the Garden.'"

Carl tensed.

Applause, applause. The curtain flew up, and the pianist plunked the introduction. Then—nothing. She began again; then nothing again.

Lorraine spun around, swatting Carl with a giant petal. "Carl! You're on . . . *sing.*"

The next few moments were a blur for Carl. What he sang, he couldn't remember. It could have been "Pop Goes the Weasel" for all he knew. But when he was through, he noticed his sister, his mom and dad, and his aunt smiling and waving and snapping pictures. So Carl smiled too and, when the scene was over, hopped off the stage—awfully glad it was over.

Many single adults can identify with Carl. In a way, they have to perform a solo every day, when they leave for work in the morning, when they come home to microwave their dinner-in-a-box, when they wonder what to do on Friday night, or when their mothers ask, "Is there anyone special?" It's easy to see why some singles would get stage fright.

One Bible character who dealt successfully with his singleness was the apostle Paul. Let's examine his photograph on this last page of our family album and discover what helped him sing out his solo.

## The One Essential Ingredient

In Paul's life, the one ingredient inspiring his positive attitude in any situation was contentment. "I have learned," he said,

> to be content in whatever circumstances I am. I know how to get along with humble means, and I also know how to live in prosperity; in any and every circumstance I have learned the secret of being filled and going hungry, both of having abundance and suffering need. (Phil. 4:11b–12)

Being content must have given Paul great inner confidence, for he was at peace whatever his circumstance: rich or poor, hungry or filled, or—we can add—married or unmarried. Contentment is also the essential ingredient for a single person's sense of satisfaction today. "Do I accept my singleness? Do I see value in my solo role? Am I at peace with myself?"

What often sets a trap for singles is thinking that marriage is the essential ingredient for happiness and a full life. But as we'll discover in this lesson, that's not necessarily true, for learning how to be content can bring fulfillment now.

## Some Insights for Single Adults

Since we live in a couple-oriented society, people often wonder what's wrong with anyone who is still single. If you're feeling that pressure, take encouragement from Scripture, which highlights the lives of several single adults.

### Some Biographical Examples to Remember

You are in good company with many of the Old Testament prophets who charted a solo course through biblical history. And you'll find friends in the New Testament as well, such as John the Baptizer and, as we mentioned, Paul—missionary to the world. Can you imagine these people having the same impact on their society if they had had to be home for supper by five-thirty and spend their weekends at tee-ball games and piano recitals? Of course, they could have married—they had that right (see 1 Cor. 9:5). Yet they chose to give that up so that, in Paul's words, they would "cause no hindrance to the gospel of Christ" (v. 12b).

Paul's example, specifically, points out four principles about singleness, which we'll examine next.

### Some Biblical Principles to Follow

First, *it is not God's plan that everyone should marry*. In fact, singleness can be a gift from God.

> But this I say by way of concession, not of command. Yet I wish that all men were even as I myself am. However, each man has his own gift from God, one in this manner, and another in that.
> But I say to the unmarried and to widows that it is good for them if they remain even as I. But if they do not have self-control, let them marry; for it is better to marry than to burn. (1 Cor. 7:6–9)

The "gift from God" has often been thought of as celibacy. As one commentator explains, those with this gift do not

> "burn in oneself" with the strong fire of sexual desire, which, deprived of marriage, may . . . in secret devastate the inner spiritual life.[1]

This sexual self-control seems to be the test of whether God has gifted a person to be single rather than married.

Later in the same chapter, the Apostle continues his instructions about singleness, from which we can infer a second principle: *personal contentment is of greater value than marital companionship*.

> Now concerning virgins I have no command of the Lord, but I give an opinion as one who by the mercy

---

1. R. C. H. Lenski, *The Interpretation of St. Paul's First and Second Epistles to the Corinthians* (Minneapolis, Minn.: Augsburg Publishing House, 1937), p. 285.

of the Lord is trustworthy.[2] I think then that this is good in view of the present distress, that it is good for a man to remain as he is. Are you bound to a wife? Do not seek to be released. Are you released from a wife? Do not seek a wife. (vv. 25–27)

Prompting these commands was the persecution under Nero that Paul saw coming. By remaining as they were, the people could better cope with the coming distress. As David K. Lowery observes,

however fearsome the thought of martyrdom . . . might be to a single person, it was doubly so to a married person responsible for a spouse and children. With these conditions in view marriage would not be wrong . . . , but it would be inexpedient.[3]

Underlying Paul's words is the theme of contentment. "Do not seek . . . Do not seek . . ." (v. 27). He's saying, "Be content in your present situation rather than making rash changes out of panic." For the single person, the implication is, "If you do not find peace with yourself now, it's very doubtful you will find it in marriage." In other words, personal contentment is the foundation upon which the house of marital companionship is built.

As Paul elaborates on why this foundation is necessary, we find another principle: *marriage, while not sinful, is extremely difficult to maintain.*

But if you should marry, you have not sinned; and if a virgin should marry, she has not sinned. Yet such will have trouble in this life, and I am trying to spare you. . . . I want you to be free from concern. (vv. 28, 32a)

The Apostle does not want his readers to misunderstand him; he is not against marriage, but he realizes that along with marriage come unique challenges that singles don't have to face. Like weights on a hiker's backpack, these challenges may slow the married person's spiritual progress—weights such as adjusting to another's habits, rearing children, or handling family duties.

2. Paul is not saying his instructions are uninspired, only that Christ said nothing directly about this matter and that his counsel is in concert with Christ's own commands.

3. David K. Lowery, "1 Corinthians," in *The Bible Knowledge Commentary*, New Testament ed. (Wheaton, Ill.: Scripture Press Publications, Victor Books, 1983), p. 519.

With a lighter pack of responsibilities, the single person can walk with the Lord freer from "concern." The word Paul uses is *amerimnos*, which literally means "un-worried."[4] Also, according to A. T. Robertson, this word is related to *merizō*, which means "divide" (see v. 34).[5] The implication is that Christian singles have fewer cares that might divide their interests and weigh them down on their spiritual journey.

In verses 32b–35, we find a closely related principle: *being single, while not ideal, can be spiritually profitable.*

> One who is unmarried is concerned about the things of the Lord, how he may please the Lord; but one who is married is concerned about the things of the world, how he may please his wife, and his interests are divided. And the woman who is unmarried, and the virgin, is concerned about the things of the Lord, that she may be holy both in body and spirit; but one who is married is concerned about the things of the world, how she may please her husband. And this I say for your own benefit; not to put a restraint upon you, but to promote what is seemly, and to secure undistracted devotion to the Lord.

Paul is saying to the single, "Use this time in your life to pursue holiness and undistracted devotion to the Lord." How opposite from Madison Avenue's neon message—"Pursue pleasure and undistracted devotion to *self.*" Longing to numb the pain of loneliness, many buy into this empty philosophy. Or, longing for the greener grass of marriage, they make a rash decision that leaves them with a lifetime of frustration.

So what's the answer? Live life to the fullest and make the most of your freedom in serving the Lord *now!* If the Lord blesses you in the future with a spouse, distractions will come. Suddenly, and rightly so, your time will not be your own. But now's your chance to read, to grow, to travel, to give yourself in wholehearted devotion to Christ. Don't let this opportunity go to waste!

---

4. The word is a combination of the word *merimna*, "anxiety or worry," and the *a* prefix, which negates the word—"un-worried."

5. "The verb *merimnaō* is from *meris, merizō* [to divide], because care or anxiety distracts and divides." Archibald Thomas Robertson, *Word Pictures in the New Testament* (Grand Rapids, Mich.: Baker Book House, 1930), vol. 1, p. 58.

### Some Practical Counsel to Heed

Let's package all we've said into some words of advice. First, to marrieds, *instead of resisting, start respecting*. Remember five-year-old Carl? What encouraged him most while performing his solo was his family cheering him on. The greatest way you can cheer on the single people you know is by respecting them. Marriage may not be in God's plan for them. Or maybe God wants them to wait for His person in His time. Show respect by accepting singles as they are and letting God do the matchmaking.

Second, to singles, *instead of drifting and doubting, start pursuing*. Content in who you are and confident in God's abilities within you, run to the Lord. Devote yourself to knowing Him fully. Wring out every ounce of life He gives you. For, in the words of one writer,

> this day will never come again and anyone who fails to eat and drink and taste and smell it will never have it offered to him again in all eternity. The sun will never shine as it does today . . . you must play your part and sing a song, one of your best.[6]

So, Carl . . . sing out!

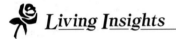 *Living Insights*

What better person to speak to singles than a single person? Luci Swindoll, Chuck's sister, concludes her book *Wide My World, Narrow My Bed*, with this vibrant advice.

> My dear, single friends—if I could close this book with one ringing message in your ears, it would be once again to encourage you to get into the enthusiasm of living. Don't wait for a mate. Don't wait for more time. Don't wait until you have more money. Don't wait until both your feet are on the ground. Don't wait for *anything else*. The time to be involved with living is now—not tomorrow or next week or next year. Now.

---

6. Hermann Hesse, *Klingsor's Last Summer*, trans. Richard and Clara Winston (New York, N.Y.: Farrar, Straus and Giroux, 1970), as quoted by Luci Swindoll in *Wide My World, Narrow My Bed* (Portland, Oreg.: Multnomah Press, 1982), p. 75.

You say, "There are so many problems with being single. I'm lonely, I'm bored, I don't know how to enjoy things by myself." Of course there are problems. There are problems in any lifestyle, because that is part of the living process. . . .

I would venture to say many of your problems as a single person exist because you are holding back. You're waiting for something better to come along, that certain something that will enrich your circumstances. Well, friends—it's here. It's called Life. And Breath. And God. That's all you need. You don't have to be married to be happy. You just have to be alive.[7]

If you feel like you need to reconnect with God's adventurous plan for your life, here are a few suggestions and some space for you to brainstorm your own ideas.

Get involved in volunteer work in your community.
Join a short-term missionary team.
Every day, do something to improve your health.
Unplug the TV for a week and rediscover yourself.
Plan a trip with a friend.
Start a children's Bible club.
Welcome laughter into your life.
Learn sign language.
Take a class at your local college.
Spend a week with a missionary family in another country.
Take your parents out to dinner.
Write a letter to a friend.
Meditate on Scripture.
Plant a garden.

_____  _____

_____  _____

_____  _____

_____  _____

7. Swindoll, *Wide My World, Narrow My Bed*, pp. 170–71.

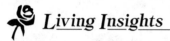 *Living Insights*

We've come to the last page of our family album. Maybe you've become acquainted with a few Bible characters you've never met before. You may have been surprised at the variety of family settings. Perhaps you've seen a little of yourself in these snapshots. Before you close the cover, glance back one last time at the people in the photographs. As you do, write down what their lives have taught you. Then use these messages to build your own museum of memories.

Jochebed _____

_____

Aquila and Priscilla _____

_____

Grandpa Uzziah _____

_____

The Son Born Blind _____

_____

The Widow of Zarephath _____

_____

The Prodigal Son's Father _____

_____

Esther _____

_____

Paul _____

_____

INSIGHT FOR LIVING

# A FAMILY ALBUM

Today's family often goes beyond the typical family unit of husband and wife, children and parents; it sometimes includes a blend of single parents, adopted children, grandparents, and aunts and uncles. The following books are recommended reading on the challenges facing today's ever-changing families.

**The Future of the American Family**—In this book, George Barna summarizes his research on cultural and social changes affecting the family in America. He supplements his narrative with statistics and charts. This is a resource for parents and educators who want to understand why we have a family crisis in America, where the family is headed, and what we can do to develop stronger families.

**Successful Single Parenting**—This book is the total resource for today's single parent. It presents facts and figures and down-to-earth practical ideas for the parent who is going it alone. Gary Richmond discusses problems and solutions that, with God's help, can make life more joyful and secure. He offers counsel and encouragement to help the single parent preserve that crucial sense of still being a family.

**Loving Someone Else's Child**—If God has brought a child into your life and you are filling the role of stepparent, guardian, godparent, teacher, coach, Big Brother, foster parent, grandparent, aunt, uncle, youth pastor, father figure, or friend, this book is for you. Angela Elwell Hunt effectively communicates the challenges and rewards of loving children beyond your own.

**Parents, Pregnant Teens and the Adoption Option**—Jeanne Warren Lindsay defines *birthgrandparent* as "one who loses a grandchild through adoption." This book captures the feelings, fears, and hopes of all birthgrandparents who feel alone and without support as their daughter (or son) faces a too-early pregnancy and the difficult adoption/keeping decision.

# ORDER FORM

This special offer expires February 28, 1994.

| Title | California | U.S. | Canada | Quantity | Amount |
|---|---|---|---|---|---|
| *The Future of the American Family* (**FUAHB**) (hardcover) | $18.45 | $17.20 | $23.20 | _____ | $_____ |
| *Successful Single Parenting* (**SSPPB**) (softcover) | 8.69 | 8.10 | 10.95 | _____ | _____ |
| *Loving Someone Else's Child* (**LSCPB**) (softcover) | 9.76 | 9.10 | 12.30 | _____ | _____ |
| *Parents, Pregnant Teens and Adoption* (**PPTPB**) (softcover) | 9.71 | 9.05 | 12.20 | _____ | _____ |

Subtotal  $_____

For faster shipping, United States residents can add
10 percent for first-class shipping and handling.  _____

Contribution to the Insight for Living radio ministry.  _____
*All contributions are tax-deductible.*

**Total Amount Enclosed**  $_____
*Check or money order should be made payable to Insight for Living.*

**These prices have been discounted 10 percent from retail price. All prices include applicable taxes and shipping costs.**

---

Credit card purchases: ❑ Visa  ❑ MasterCard  ❑ Discover Card

Expiration Date _____  Number _____

Signature _____
*We cannot process your credit card purchase without your signature.*

For credit card orders, you are welcome to use one of our toll-free numbers between the hours of 7:00 A.M. and 4:30 P.M., Pacific time, Monday through Friday, or our FAX numbers. The numbers to use from anywhere in the United States are **1-800-772-8888** or FAX (714) 575-5496. To order from Canada, call our Vancouver office using **1-800-663-7639** or FAX (604) 596-2975. Vancouver residents, call (604) 596-2910.

Name _____

Address _____

City _____

State/Province _____  Zip/Postal Code _____

Country _____

Telephone ( _____ ) _____  Radio Station ___ ___ ___ ___
*If questions arise concerning your order, we may need to contact you.*

Insight for Living • Post Office Box 69000, Anaheim, CA 92817-0900
Insight for Living Ministries • Post Office Box 2510, Vancouver, BC, Canada V6B 3W7
*Please allow four to six weeks for delivery.*

# BOOKS FOR
# PROBING FURTHER

O ver coffee, two friends talked about their lives and families. "This book has been very helpful to me," said one. "Why don't you read it and let me know what you think?"

"Thanks, I think I will," replied the other, as the book passed from hand to hand.

With that same expression of friendship, we offer you the following resources. Pick one that fits, read it, and let us know what you think. We'll keep the coffee brewing.

## Motherhood

Balswick, Judith, with Lynn Brookside. *Mothers and Daughters Making Peace*. Ann Arbor, Mich.: Servant Publications, Vine Books, 1993.

Chall, Sally Leman. *Mommy Appleseed: Planting Seeds of Faith in the Heart of Your Child*. Eugene, Oreg.: Harvest House Publishers, 1993.

Lush, Jean, with Pamela Vredevelt. *Mothers and Sons*. Old Tappan, N.J.: Fleming H. Revell Co., 1988.

## Couple Power

Jacks, Bob and Betty. *Your Home, a Lighthouse*. Rev. ed. Colorado Springs, Colo.: NavPress, 1987.

Love, Vicky. *Childless Is Not Less*. Minneapolis, Minn: Bethany House Publishers, 1984.

## Grandparenting

Bly, Stephen and Janet. *How to Be a Good Grandparent*. Chicago, Ill.: Moody Press, 1990.

## Parenting the Disabled

Cook, Rosemarie S. *Parenting a Child with Special Needs*. Grand Rapids, Mich.: Zondervan Publishing House, 1992.

Newman, Gene, and Joni Eareckson Tada. *All God's Children:*

*Ministry with Disabled Persons*. Rev. ed. Grand Rapids, Mich.: Zondervan Publishing House, 1993.

## Single Parenting

Aldrich, Sandra Picklesimer. *From One Single Mother to Another*. Ventura, Calif.: Gospel Light Publications, Regal Books, 1991.

Richmond, Gary. *Successful Single Parenting*. Eugene, Oreg.: Harvest House Publishers, 1990.

## Fatherhood

Canfield, Ken R. *The 7 Secrets of Effective Fathers*. Wheaton, Ill.: Tyndale House Publishers, 1992.

Johnson, Greg, and Mike Yorkey. *"Daddy's Home": A Practical Guide for Maximizing the Most Important Hours of Your Day*. Wheaton, Ill.: Tyndale House Publishers, 1992.

## Adoption

*A Loving Choice* booklet. Grand Rapids, Mich.: Bethany Productions, 1990.

*Letting Go*. Videotape for birthparents. *More Than Love*. Videotape for adoptive families. Bethany Productions, 901 Eastern Ave. NE, Grand Rapids, MI 49503-1295, (616) 459-6273. Recommended for private counseling or in-home viewing.

Schooler, Jayne E. *The Whole Life Adoption Book*. Colorado Springs, Colo.: Piñon Press, 1993.

## Singleness

Mossholder, Ray. *Singles Plus: The Bible and Being Single*. Lake Mary, Fla.: Creation House, 1991.

All of the books listed above are recommended reading; however, some may be out of print and available only through a library. For books currently available, please contact your local Christian bookstore. Works by Charles R. Swindoll are available through Insight for Living. IFL also offers some books by other authors— please note the Ordering Information that follows and contact the office that serves you.

# ORDERING INFORMATION

## Cassette Tapes and Study Guide

This Bible study guide was designed to be used independently or in conjunction with the broadcast of Chuck Swindoll's taped messages on the topic listed below. If you would like to order cassette tapes or further copies of this study guide, please see the information given below and the Order Form provided at the end of this guide.

### A FAMILY ALBUM

What treasure is in a family album! Every photograph is a priceless heirloom with a story all its own. A grandfather reads to his admiring grandson, a single mom stands arm in arm with her daughters, or a dad tenderly holds his newly adopted baby.

In God's family album—the Bible—the pictures tell equally touching stories. The members of His family that we'll meet in this study include Moses' mother, an openhearted husband-and-wife team, a prideful grandfather, a disabled man, a struggling single parent, a model dad, an adopted orphan, and a single adult.

So crawl up on your Father's lap and let Him turn the pages and tell the stories of some of your spiritual ancestors. It will be a time to treasure.

|  |  | Calif.* | U.S. | B.C.* | Canada* |
|---|---|---|---|---|---|
| FAM CS | Cassette series, includes album cover | $31.32 | $29.20 | $39.30 | $36.75 |
| FAM 1–4 | Individual cassettes, includes messages A and B | 6.76 | 6.30 | 8.95 | 8.50 |
| FAM SG | Study guide | 4.24 | 3.95 | 5.25 | 5.25 |

*These prices already include the following charges: for delivery in **California**, applicable sales tax; **Canada**, 7% GST and 7% postage and handling (on tapes only); **British Columbia**, 7% GST, 6% British Columbia sales tax (on tapes only), and 7% postage and handling (on tapes only). **The prices are subject to change without notice.**

FAM  1-A: *Meet the Mother of Moses*—Exodus 1:8–2:10
        B: *A Couple Mightily Used of God*—Acts 18:1–3, 18–21, 24–28

FAM  2-A: *"Grandpa Uzziah": A Study in Contrasts*—
          2 Chronicles 26:1–21
        B: *The Parents of a Son Born Blind*—John 9

FAM  3-A: *A Double Blessing for a Single Parent*—1 Kings 17
        B: *Earning the Right to Be Called "Dad"*—Luke 15:11–32

**FAM  4-A:** *From Captive to Queen: An Adoption Story*—
The Book of Esther
   **B:** *If You Have the Solo . . . Sing Out!*—
1 Corinthians 7:6–9, 25–35

## How to Order by Mail

Simply mark on the order form whether you want the series or individual tapes. Mail the form with your payment to the appropriate address listed below. We will process your order as promptly as we can.

**United States:** Mail your order to the Ordering Services Department at Insight for Living, Post Office Box 69000, Anaheim, California 92817-0900. If you wish your order to be shipped first-class for faster delivery, add 10 percent of the total order amount. Otherwise, please allow four to six weeks for delivery by fourth-class mail. We accept payment by personal check, money order, or credit card. Unfortunately, we are unable to offer invoicing or COD orders.

**Note:** To cover processing and handling, there is a $10 fee for *any* returned check.

**Canada:** Mail your order to Insight for Living Ministries, Post Office Box 2510, Vancouver, British Columbia V6B 3W7. Allow approximately four weeks for delivery. We accept payment by personal check, money order, or credit card. Unfortunately, we are unable to offer invoicing or COD orders.

**Australia, New Zealand, or Papua New Guinea:** Mail your order to Insight for Living, Inc., GPO Box 2823 EE, Melbourne, Victoria 3001, Australia. Please allow six to ten weeks for delivery by surface mail. If you would like your order sent airmail, the delivery time may be reduced. Using the United States price as a base, add postage costs—surface or airmail— to the amount of your order. Please use the chart that follows to determine correct postage. Due to fluctuating currency rates, we can accept only personal checks made payable in United States funds, international money orders, or credit cards in payment for materials.

**Overseas:** Other overseas residents should mail their orders to our United States office. Please allow six to ten weeks for delivery by surface mail. If you would like your order sent airmail, the delivery time may be reduced. Using the United States price as a base, add postage costs— surface or airmail—to the amount of your order. Please use the chart that follows to determine correct postage. Due to fluctuating currency rates, we can accept only personal checks made payable in United States funds, international money orders, or credit cards in payment for materials.

| Type of Postage | Postage Cost |
| --- | --- |
| Surface | 10% of total order |
| Airmail | 25% of total order |

## For Faster Service, Order by Telephone or FAX

For credit card orders, you are welcome to use one of our toll-free numbers between the hours of 7:00 A.M. and 4:30 P.M., Pacific time, Monday through Friday, or our FAX numbers. The numbers to use from anywhere in the United States are **1-800-772-8888** or FAX (714) 575-5496. To order from Canada, call our Vancouver office using **1-800-663-7639** or FAX (604) 596-2975. Vancouver residents, call (604) 596-2910. Australian residents should phone (03) 872-4606. From other international locations, call our Ordering Services Department at (714) 575-5000 in the United States.

## Our Guarantee

Your complete satisfaction is our top priority here at Insight for Living. If you're not completely satisfied with anything you order, please return it for full credit, a refund, or a replacement, as *you* prefer.

## Insight for Living Catalog

Request a free copy of the Insight for Living catalog of books, tapes, and study guides by calling **1-800-772-8888** in the United States or **1-800-663-7639** in Canada.

# Order Form

FAM CS represents the entire *A Family Album* series in a special album cover, while FAM 1–4 are the individual tapes included in the series. FAM SG represents this study guide, should you desire to order additional copies.

| Item | Calif.* | Unit Price U.S. | B.C.* | Canada* | Quantity | Amount |
|------|---------|------|-------|---------|----------|--------|
| FAM CS | $31.32 | $29.20 | $39.30 | $36.75 | | $ |
| FAM 1 | 6.76 | 6.30 | 8.95 | 8.50 | | |
| FAM 2 | 6.76 | 6.30 | 8.95 | 8.50 | | |
| FAM 3 | 6.76 | 6.30 | 8.95 | 8.50 | | |
| FAM 4 | 6.76 | 6.30 | 8.95 | 8.50 | | |
| FAM SG | 4.24 | 3.95 | 5.25 | 5.25 | | |
| | | | | | **Subtotal** | |
| | | | | | **Overseas Residents** *Pay U.S. price plus 10% surface postage or 25% airmail. Also, see "How to Order by Mail."* | |
| | | | | | **U.S. First-Class Shipping** *For faster delivery, add 10% for postage and handling.* | |
| | | | | | **Gift to Insight for Living** *Tax-deductible in the United States and Canada.* | |
| | | | | | **Total Amount Due** *Please do not send cash.* | $ |

If there is a balance: ❑ Apply it as a donation ❑ Please refund
*These prices already include applicable taxes and shipping costs.

**Payment by:** ❑ Check or money order payable to Insight for Living ❑ Credit card

(Circle one): Visa MasterCard Discover Card Number_____

Expiration Date_____ Signature_____
*We cannot process your credit card purchase without your signature.*

Name_____

Address_____

City_____ State/Province_____

Zip/Postal Code_____ Country_____

Telephone (___)_____ Radio Station____ ____ ____ ____
*If questions arise concerning your order, we may need to contact you.*

**Mail this order form to the Ordering Services Department at one of these addresses:**
Insight for Living, Post Office Box 69000, Anaheim, CA 92817-0900
Insight for Living Ministries, Post Office Box 2510, Vancouver, BC, Canada V6B 3W7
Insight for Living, Inc., GPO Box 2823 EE, Melbourne, VIC 3001, Australia